Foolproof Guide to Growing
Roses

CREATIVE
HOMEOWNER®

Foolproof Guide to Growing
Roses

CREATIVE HOMEOWNER®, Upper Saddle River, New Jersey

A Division of Federal Marketing Corp.
Upper Saddle River, NJ 07458

Editorial Director: Timothy O. Bakke
Art Director: Monduane Harris
Production Manager: Kimberly H. Vivas

Editors: Miranda Smith, Nancy Engel, Heidi Stonehill
Copy Editor: Ellie Sweeney
Photo Researchers: Stanley Sudol, Amla Sanghvi
Proofreaders: Sharon Ranftle, Ellie Sweeney
Editorial Assistants: Sharon Ranftle, Dan Lane, Dan Houghtaling
Indexer: Ellen Davenport

Front Cover Designer: Monduane Harris
Back Cover Designer: Charles Van Vooren
Interior Book Designers: Virginia Wells Blaker, Charles Van Vooren
Illustrator: Mavis Torke
Front Cover Photographer: John Glover
Back Cover Photographers: Field Roebuck, top, Jerry Pavia, bottom

Printed in the United States of America

Current Printing (last digit)
10 9 8 7 6 5 4 3

Library of Congress Catalog Card Number: 00-111620
ISBN: 1580110835

CREATIVE HOMEOWNER®
A Division of Federal Marketing Corp.
24 Park Way
Upper Saddle River, NJ 07458
www.creativehomeowner.com

Metric Equivalents

All measurements in this book are given in U.S. Customary units. If you wish to find metric equivalents, use the following tables and conversion factors.

Inches to Millimeters and Centimeters

1 in = 25.4 mm = 2.54 cm

in	mm	cm
1/16	1.5875	0.1588
1/8	3.1750	0.3175
1/4	6.3500	0.6350
3/8	9.5250	0.9525
1/2	12.7000	1.2700
5/8	15.8750	1.5875
3/4	19.0500	1.9050
7/8	22.2250	2.2225
1	25.4000	2.5400

Inches to Centimeters and Meters

1 in = 2.54 cm = 0.0254 m

in	cm	m
1	2.54	0.0254
2	5.08	0.0508
3	7.62	0.0762
4	10.16	0.1016
5	12.70	0.1270
6	15.24	0.1524
7	17.78	0.1778
8	20.32	0.2032
9	22.86	0.2286
10	25.40	0.2540
11	27.94	0.2794
12	30.48	0.3048

Feet to Meters

1 ft = 0.3048 m

ft	m
1	0.3048
5	1.5240
10	3.0480
25	7.6200
50	15.2400
100	30.4800

Square Feet to Square Meters

1 ft^2 = 0.092 903 04 m^2

Acres to Square Meters

1 acre = 4046.85642 m^2

Cubic Yards to Cubic Meters

1 yd^3 = 0.764 555 m^3

Ounces and Pounds (Avoirdupois) to Grams

1 oz = 28.349 523 g

1 lb = 453.5924 g

Pounds to Kilograms

1 lb = 0.453 592 37 kg

Ounces and Quarts to Liters

1 oz = 0.029 573 53 L

1 qt = 0.9463 L

Gallons to Liters

1 gal = 3.785 411 784 L

Fahrenheit to Celsius (Centigrade)

$°C = °F - 32 \times \frac{5}{9}$

°F	°C
-30	-34.45
-20	-28.89
-10	-23.34
-5	-20.56
0	-17.78
10	-12.22
20	-6.67
30	-1.11
32 (freezing)	0.00
40	4.44
50	10.00
60	15.56
70	21.11
80	26.67
90	32.22
100	37.78
212 (boiling)	100

Safety First

All projects and procedures in this book have been reviewed for safety. Still, it is not possible to overstate the importance of working carefully. Here are some reminders for plant care and project safety. Always use common sense.

Always determine locations of underground utility lines before you dig; and then avoid them by a safe distance. Buried lines may be for gas, electricity, communications, or water. Start research by contacting your local building officials. Also contact local utility companies. They will often send a representative at no cost to help you map the lines.

Always read and heed tool manufacturer instructions, especially the warnings.

Always ensure that the electrical setup is safe. Be sure that no circuit is overloaded and that all power tools and electrical outlets are properly grounded and protected by a ground-fault circuit interrupter (GFCI). Do not use power tools in wet locations.

Always wear eye protection when using chemicals, sawing wood, pruning trees and shrubs, using power tools, and striking metal onto metal or concrete.

Always consider nontoxic and least-toxic methods of addressing unwanted plants, plant pests, and plant diseases before resorting to toxic methods. When selecting among toxic substances, consider short-lived toxins that break down quickly into harmless substances. Follow package applications and safety instructions carefully.

Always read labels on chemicals, solvents, and other products; provide ventilation; and heed warnings.

Always wear protective clothing, including a face mask and gloves, when working with toxic materials.

Never use herbicides, pesticides, or other toxic chemicals unless you have determined with certainty that they were developed for the specific problem you hope to remedy.

Never work with power tools when you are tired or under the influence of alcohol or drugs.

Never carry sharp or pointed tools, such as knives or saws, in your pockets.

Table of Contents

The rose has been the most cherished garden flower for all of recorded history, according to archaeological evidence. Achilles used the rose as an emblem on his shield, and the island of Rhodes made the rose its symbol.

Roses and depictions of rose flowers were found in the tombs of the ancient Egyptians, on clay tablets at Ur of the Chaldees in ancient Mesopotamia, and in frescoes at the palace of Knossos on Crete. Roses grew in the Hanging Gardens of Babylon and at King Solomon's Temple in Jerusalem. Worshipers at the Temple of Aphrodite on the Greek island of Samos and Medean fire worshipers in ancient Persia revered roses. Sappho, the Greek poetess, wrote about them in roughly 600 B.C. During the Middle Ages, roses were primarily in the care of monks and apothecaries, who grew them in gardens with other medicinal plants. But by the end of this period, the rose had regained its rightful place—elaborate rose gardens graced

European parks, castles, chateaux, and manor-house grounds. The burgeoning middle class also grew roses. Thus was born the concept of modern rose gardens, which can be large or small and are adaptable even to the humblest of abodes.

This love of roses has become a part of the psyche of almost every gardener. But many modern gardeners believe that growing roses is too much trouble and requires too much work. Others go ahead and plant roses but then do their very best to confirm that belief. They spend hours every weekend watering, trimming, deadheading, raking debris, plucking infected leaflets, and spraying their roses with an entire arsenal of chemical weapons. Sadly, both types of gardeners are missing out on the real pleasures of roses and rose gardening, and both are suffering from mistaken impressions about roses.

As we have seen, roses have been cultivated for thousands of years. But neither ancient peoples nor our pioneer ancestors had enough free time to spend hours every week—or even hours every month—laboring over their roses. Nor did they have captan or Diazinon. Widespread use of chemical warfare in the garden has come about mostly since the 1940s.

Hundreds of varieties of Old Garden Roses have grown on their own for decades at a time, completely unattended in some neglected cemetery or next to an abandoned farmhouse. And many modern varieties are proving themselves to be just as robust and healthy.

By choosing appropriate, easy-care varieties and using the proper cultural practices, you can grow beautiful roses in your garden and in your landscape—without engaging in time-consuming and expensive chemical warfare that's not only detrimental to the environment but also potentially damaging to your own well-being. You will also discover that growing roses without chemicals can result in a lot more gardening pleasure and personal satisfaction. This book tells you how to go about it.

CHAPTER ONE

Types and Uses of Roses

Roses are the most varied and versatile of all landscape plants because of the many species and huge number of individual cultivars. If you were to search through all the roses for sale at nurseries, garden and home centers, and in mail-order catalogs from Europe, Canada, and the United States, you'd discover well over 13,000 named cultivars. Growers add to this number every year when they introduce hundreds of new cultivars. Thanks to this wealth, you have a truly amazing choice of flower color and form as well as plant size and habit. You can find a rose to suit almost any spot in the landscape.

▲ **Rosa rugosa**

◄ **Climbing roses** *add a note of elegance to any garden.*
Grow them on trellises, arches, pillars, or espaliered on walls.

Colors and Forms

Rose flower colors vary from pristine white to deep purple. The only color that doesn't appear naturally is a true "delphinium blue"—that gene just doesn't exist within the rose family.

Flower forms vary from blossoms with five petals to those with 80 or more, and sizes range from $1/2$-inch-wide buttons to pom-poms as large as salad bowls. Plant sizes range from tiny shrubs less than a foot tall to gargantuan climbers with 50-foot canes.

Rose flowers are described as single, semidouble, double, or very double. Traditionally, a single rose has a single row of only 5 petals. However, some refer to flowers with up to 10 or 11 petals as singles.

Double flowers have 25 (some say 35) or more petals, and semidouble flowers have more petals than singles do but fewer than doubles. Very double roses are the pom-pomlike flowers with petals almost too numerous to count—75 or more.

Roses in the garden. Despite their diversity and versatility, many people think of roses only in the context of a flower arrangement, bouquet, or corsage. Also, many gardeners still design formal and almost sterile growing beds for their roses.

Blame It on Empress Josephine

You can blame the Empress Josephine for at least a part of the rigid designs for rose gardens. While her husband Napoleon I was off fighting, she passed the time by establishing an extensive garden of flowering plants. In addition to several other types of plants, she collected and installed at least one of every variety of rose known at the time—or at least she tried to do so. She planted her roses in neatly spaced rows in crisply formal beds, outlined with borders of square-cut boxwood.

Following her lead and not to be outdone, the lords and ladies of the manor soon established similar gardens at noble houses throughout Europe. Eventually the formal style trickled down to the masses. Thus was born the concept and design of today's "formal" rose garden. The burgeoning popularity of the darlings of today's exhibitors—first the hybrid perpetual roses and then the hybrid teas, with their high centers and formal looks—aided and abetted the adoption of this design style.

Happily, the enthusiasm for this fashion has waned somewhat; more and more, roses are taking their rightful place as useful and versatile landscape plants.

▼ **Formal gardens** *with rigid lines exemplify the style created by Empress Josephine.*

Changing Styles. Much of the credit for this design shift must go to the rediscovery of "grandmother's roses," the fragrant, shrubby roses of yesteryear—and to the more recent development of several new families of roses bred specifically for use in the home landscape. But don't confine yourself to those groups; the many types listed below can fit into many spots in a home landscape.

Miniature and Small-Size Roses

Miniature roses are an official class of roses, as designated by the American Rose Society. However, for the purposes of this discussion, miniature roses are those that grow from about 6 inches tall to no more than $1^1/2$ to 2 feet tall and wide. In contrast, some of the species officially classed as miniature roses are miniature only in flower size—the plants may be 4 feet tall and wide.

Parentage. All small-size roses descend from a diminutive form of *Rosa chinensis*, a plant that was brought to Europe from China in the early 1800s. Today, this group of plants includes all of the smaller cultivars of the miniature roses, china roses, and polyanthas. Most of them have relatively small flowers without much fragrance. In general they have thickly foliated, twiggy canes and grow into shrubs with an upright and rounded shape. If they aren't naturally rounded, it's easy to trim them to that form. Consequently, they're ideal border or edging plants, in low foundation plantings, and to give splashes of color in beds with taller shrubs and perennials.

You can also grow these smaller roses in all sorts of containers, including window boxes and hanging

▲ **Miniature roses** are ideal for hanging baskets.

▲ **Miniature roses** are also just the right size and scale for a variety of lovely planters.

◄ **Miniature roses** make excellent edging plants in many locations.

baskets. The smallest varieties—the so-called microminis that are no more than 6 or 8 inches tall—can grow for several years in a pot as small as a 1-gallon container. A 5-gallon pot is entirely adequate for a 2-foot plant. Group your containers with other plants on and around patios, porches, and balconies.

But don't think of these roses as indoor plants—not even those tiny little ones you find next to the checkout counter at the grocery store. You can overwinter roses in containers in a bright, cool place inside when it's absolutely necessary, but they should be outdoors in the sunlight whenever the temperature is above freezing. A well-watered, 5-gallon container can remain out in the elements as long as the temperature doesn't drop below 28°F for more than seven or eight hours.

Rose Classifications

The American Rose Society and the World Federation of Rose Societies classify roses according to the length of time they have been cultivated and their basic form. For a full discussion of rose classes, see pages 10 to 15.

▲ **'Cocktail'** *makes a graceful focal point in this lawn because the form of the plant is as lovely as the blooms.*

◄ **'Carefree Beauty'** *is a lush addition to any landscape. The fragrant blooms give way to decorative hips in the fall.*

Medium-Size Shrubs and Bushes

Medium–size roses range between 2 to 5 or 6 feet tall, although some cultivars can easily soar to more than 10 feet in the warmer parts of the country.

Roses of this intermediate size are generally shrubs or bushes. Shrubs are a rose class, but in this discussion the term refers to plants that have a wide rounded or urn-shaped form and branching canes. These plants also tend to retain most of their bottom foliage.

This group includes representatives of several official classes of roses, including gallicas, portlands, chinas, teas, polyanthas, bourbons, rugosas, and floribundas. (See pages 10 to 15 for a discussion of rose classes.) It also includes most of the cultivars that growers term "modern shrub roses" such as the Canadian Explorer series and newer shrubs from the growers Griffith Buck, David Austin, and Meilland.

Medium–size shrub roses make good back-of-the-border plants, stand-alone accents, foundation plants, and hedges. The especially thorny varieties form an impenetrable barrier when closely spaced.

"Bush" roses differ from shrubs in that they are more upright and gangly and tend—after a couple of seasons, at least—to lose their lower leaves and become bare-legged. Hybrid perpetuals, hybrid teas, grandifloras, and some of the leggier floribundas qualify as bush types.

Use these roses in formal rose gardens, where their bare-legged appearance is expected. Plant them in neatly

◄ **Rosa pimpinellifolia 'Grandiflora'** *makes a lovely hedge. This cultivar is less bristly and comes in lighter colors than the standard pimpinel-lifolia.*

spaced rows, reminiscent of Napoleon's grenadiers marching into battle, or hide their bare and thorny legs by putting them at the back of a bed or surrounding them with other shrubs, ornamental grasses, ground covers, or flowering perennials and annuals.

Any of the midsize roses grow well in containers, but this is particularly true of some of the hybrid teas. In pots they seem to have fewer problems with fungal diseases and often flower more lavishly, especially in parts of the country where the temperature during midsummer nights remains at 80°F or higher.

Smaller varieties of both bush- and shrub-type roses grow well in 5-gallon pots, while even the largest culti-vars in these groups grow well in whiskey barrels or 20-gallon boxes. However, in areas where the winter temperature falls below 25°F and stays there for more than 18 to 24 hours, you must move even the largest container to a protected, frost-free spot.

Large Shrubs and Small Climbers

This group of plants includes representatives of almost every official rose class — shrub types that are reputed to grow to a height from 6 to 10 feet, roses that are referred to as small climbers, and those that throw up stiff, arching canes as much as 10 to 12 feet in length. The only classes or types not included are the shrub-type miniatures, the polyanthas, and one or two types of small, modern shrub roses.

These are the transition roses — those between the true shrubs and the large climbers in size. You can use them in many ways. They make good hedges as well as freestanding accent shrubs. You can also spread the canes of the long-caned varieties — bourbons, hybrid perpet-uals, hybrid rugosas, and hybrid musks — out in a circle,

Pegging a Rose

DIFFICULTY LEVEL: MODERATE

TOOLS AND MATERIALS: Pruning shears, metal plant staples or 9-gauge wire, wire snips

1 *In early spring when the canes are green and supple, bend them to spread in a circle. Secure them in place with commercially available metal staples or pieces of 9-gauge wire.*

2 *Keep the area between the canes free of weeds. Mulch with chipped hardwood bark to give the planting a finished look and to discourage new weed growth.*

like the spokes of a wagon wheel. Peg them to the ground, and your rose will resemble a large colorful pinwheel. Pegged plants often develop flowering shoots along their outspread arms, much more so than when they are left to grow in an upright position.

Most large shrub roses make good low climbers for growing up and along walls and fences, on trellises and gazebos, and over pergolas and arches. They are also good pillar roses. Twine them around a vertical post or narrow-based tripod or tower. Several of the long-caned miniature roses, such as 'Jackie' and 'Pink Cameo', grow well in containers and hanging baskets and are excellent climbers or pillar roses.

A shrub rose can throw up canes as much as 50 percent longer than normal when it is trained and grown as a climber. For example, a shrub that might grow to 6 feet tall when freestanding reaches 8 to 10 feet tall when it is supported on a fence or trellis. As a result, you can consider some of the more robust medium-size plants, such as 'Compassion', short climbers when they are trellised and supported as climbers. This is particularly true in warmer regions where little or no wood is lost to freezing weather during the winter.

◄ **'New Dawn'** climbing roses drape over an arched trellis in this garden. After you tie the plants in place, it takes only a few hours a year to maintain them.

Climbers and Ramblers

There is no such thing as a climbing rose — at least not in the sense of a vine being a climbing plant. Roses cannot climb by themselves because they don't have tendrils to wrap around a support or holdfasts that cling to a wall or other surface. To grow a rose as a climber, you must give its canes a support of some sort and then tie them in place at close intervals.

The roses we describe as climbers are shrubs that have exceedingly long, usually thick and stiff canes. In fact, rather than being separate types, many of them are long-caned *sports*, or natural mutations, of shrub or bush roses.

Ramblers have thinner, more supple canes than climbers do, and they develop more new canes every year. Most ramblers flower only once a year, while the majority of climbing roses are repeat-blooming plants.

Climbing roses can be noisettes, tea roses, large-

◄ *Climbing roses* are excellent as espaliers.

◄ *'Oskar Cordel'*
is an antique
repeat bloomer.
Most rose cultivars
developed since
the early 1800s
bloom more than
once during the
season, but some
antiques bloom
only once, usually
in late spring or
early summer.

flowered climbers or sports of chinas, bourbons, hybrid teas, grandifloras, and floribundas. Ramblers include many species roses as well as hybrids of the naturally rambling *Rosa wichurana* and *Rosa laevigata* species.

Planting locations. Grow climbers on any strong support—fences, trellises, pillars, and even walls. Many ramblers can grow through trees, and they're ideal for ground covers or for cascading over retaining walls.

Both climbers and the stronger-caned ramblers can grow as freestanding shrubs. Give them plenty of space to sprawl, and they will form lovely tall, rounded mounds of arching canes. As an added bonus, the local birds, to say nothing of Br'er Rabbit, find safe haven in their prickly branches.

No matter where you grow climbers or ramblers, you must keep them well pruned and trimmed. Otherwise, their strong canes can bring down their support or smother a tree.

Once-Blooming and Repeat-Blooming Roses

Most of the rose cultivars developed since the early 1800s bloom repeatedly or at least twice during the season.

Other roses bloom only once a year, generally early in the season. These once-blooming roses include the old European roses and many of their hybrids, species roses, most ramblers, and—for all practical purposes—many of the climbing sports of modern shrub and bush roses. For all practical purposes, some cultivars of otherwise repeat-blooming roses bloom well only once a season when grown in Zones 8 to 10.

Most gardeners favor repeat-blooming roses, and some absolutely refuse to grow once-blooming roses. Oddly, though, while insisting that their roses must flower repeatedly, they still plant lilacs, forsythias, azaleas, spireas, peonies, wisterias and other deciduous, once-blooming shrubs and perennials.

Once-blooming roses have fully as many flowers as any repeat-blooming plant—they just do it all at the same time. Consequently, few sights are as glorious as a healthy, once-blooming rose in full flower. They're certainly worth including in any landscape or rose garden.

If you're bothered by a rose that doesn't bloom again after its big show in late spring or early summer, simply plant it among several repeat-blooming roses or with other long-flowering plants. You can use it where you can consider it just another foliage plant when it's not in bloom. But try to avoid planting several once-blooming roses in a single group unless it's as a hedge or some other sort of thorny barrier.

Smart Tip

Container Companions

Roses don't mind a bit if you add low-growing or trailing plants to their containers. Add English ivy (*Hedera helix*) for interesting and colorful foliage. Choose moss rose (*Portulaca grandiflora*) or trailing petunia for a colorful cascade and vinca for a lovely carpet.

◄ **Tree roses** *always add a note of formality to the garden no matter where they grow.*

Tree Roses

Tree roses, or standards, have an overall appearance not unlike that of a miniature palm tree — or a very large lollipop. The four conventional and common sizes of tree roses have stems that are 18, 24, 36, or 48 inches tall. Miniature tree roses are available with 12-inch stems.

Theoretically, any kind of rose can be grafted to the top of a stem or trunk, but growers most often use polyanthas, hybrid teas, and floribundas. Growers select different cultivars for the stems and roots. For example, one prominent grower uses 'Dr. Huey' for a rootstock and then buds, or grafts, an 1845 hybrid multiflora, 'De la Grifferaie', onto that to form the stem. Another well-known grower uses a hybrid multiflora rose for both the roots and the stem. Other growers commonly use rugosa roses for the stem because of their tolerance to extremely cold temperatures.

Protect your plants. Tree roses are more delicate than other roses, mostly because of the exposed stem, a bud union on the top of the stem, and sometimes another bud union at the base. Consequently, you'll need to protect the stem from freezing temperatures and from excessive top weight, accidental blows, and strong winds that might damage it or even cause it to snap in two. Because of these requirements, most gardeners find that tree roses grow best in containers or in the ground in a protected spot in a relatively warm climate where they can get by without a lot of winter protection.

But whether you grow your tree rose in a container or plant it in the ground, always keep its stem or trunk tied to the wooden supporting stake that came with it. Trim the flowering top growth regularly so that it never becomes too heavy for the stem to support.

Tree roses make a strong architectural statement wherever they grow but are particularly effective for flanking doorways, lining walks, and placing around patios, porches, and terraces. You can use them as vertical accents in the midst of a container-plant grouping on a patio or balcony. When they are set among masses of lower-growing bedding plants, their colorful waving flowers hover above the multicolored blanket below.

Definitions and Classifications

Some gardeners prefer to grow long-stemmed "hybrid" roses — those with flowers that look as if they could be included in a bouquet from the corner florist. Others prefer a garden of modern shrub roses. Still others are enamored with the antique, old garden roses.

But what is a Modern Rose? A "hybrid" rose? A modern shrub rose? What is an antique rose or an Old

Garden Rose? In a general sense, there is no clear-cut answer to any of these questions. But with respect to official definitions and classifications, there are very specific answers.

According to both the American Rose Society (ARS) and the World Federation of Rose Societies (WFRS), an Old Garden Rose—capitalized—is any variety or cultivar belonging to a rose class that existed in 1867. This year is the dividing line because 'La France', the rose officially accepted as the first hybrid tea, was introduced that year.

Modern Roses—capitalized—are cultivars of classes that came into being after 1867. Hybrid teas, floribundas, grandifloras, polyanthas, and miniatures are all Modern Roses.

If you grow exhibition roses, you must know these definitions to correctly categorize the rose you are showing as a Modern or Old Garden Rose. It's also necessary to categorize roses when you enter them into competition in any American Rose Society show.

'Souvenir de la Malmaison' *is a bourbon rose that has stood the test of time. This Old Garden Rose was named in honor of Empress Josephine's garden at Malmaison.*

However, most home gardeners don't pay much attention to the official definitions when they select plants for their rose garden or landscape. Instead, they are likely to separate modern and antique roses on the basis of their overall characteristics rather than by the date when rosarians recognized the rose type as a distinct and particular class. Beyond that, deciding whether or not a particular cultivar qualifies as an antique, old garden rose—not capitalized—or as a modern rose—not capitalized—is much like deciding if you're rich—it's as much a state of mind as anything else.

'Iceberg' *is a floribunda, a Modern Rose. It won the Royal National Rose Society Gold Medal in 1958 and is still popular today.*

Hybrid Roses

The term "hybrid rose" doesn't refer to either an official or unofficial class. Nor is it even meaningful because, except for the true species, all roses are hybrids—very complex hybrids in most cases, but hybrids nonetheless.

'Centifolia' *is the first known member of this class and the parent of the cultivars now classified as centifolia roses.*

'Fleurzauber', a gallica rose, is an Old Garden Rose that is still grown for its lovely form and color.

Old Garden Roses from Europe

There are 15 classes of Old Garden Roses, plus two miscellaneous categories for species hybrids and those roses that just don't fit anywhere else according to the official ARS definition—roses that were developed or known before 1867. Five of these classes are subdivided into climbing and nonclimbing types.

Four classes of Old Garden Roses include the old European garden roses, the romantic roses pictured in antique oil paintings—the albas, damasks, gallicas, and centifolia (Provence or cabbage) roses.

A fifth class is the family of moss roses. Although their origin is not completely known, most rosarians believe that these roses sprang naturally (or sported) from both a centifolia and damask roses.

These roses are almost all once-flowering. Within these five classes, only one type of damask rose and a very few of the moss roses flower again after their first bloom in late spring or early summer.

Rose names. As new plants are discovered, intentionally bred, or naturally mutate, gardeners give them common names that seem to suit the particular plant or cultivar. In the case of the Old Garden Roses, the names of the classes reflect either something about their physical characteristics or something about the locale where plant explorers or other travelers found them.

Alba is Latin for white and refers to the white or pale pink color of most of the flowers. *Gallica* implies the "Rose of the Gauls," the Roman name for greater France and its people. *Centifolia* is Latin for 100 petals and refers to the fullness of the many-petaled flowers. The word damask is derived

'Kazanlik' is a damask rose with the characteristic clear pink coloration. It differs from most damasks because it is almost single rather than fully double.

'Old Blush' is believed to be the same as 'Parson's Pink China', the first China rose introduced to Europe.

Old Garden Roses from the East

According to the best records available, nine of the remaining ten classes of Old Garden Roses came from the introduction, beginning in 1752, of new species roses and their pre-existing, natural or manmade hybrids from China, Japan, and eastern India.

First came the repeat-flowering china roses, 'Parson's Pink China' and forms of 'Slater's Crimson China'. When hybridized with native species and the old European roses, they formed a class of their own, china roses.

These were crossed with the old European roses and with other species and hybrids from the Orient to yield the ayrshire, bourbon, boursault, eglanteria (sweetbriar), hybrid perpetual, portland, sempervirens, and tea rose.

The 15th official class, but by no means the last to be developed, was the noisettes, one of the few types of truly repeat-flowering climbers. This is the only official class of Old Garden Roses developed in the United States.

Of these 15 classes, only a few examples of the ayrshires, boursaults, sempervirens, and sweetbriar hybrids still exist. However, many excellent examples of the other 11 families are still around and are readily available.

from Damascus, Syria, from where the rose was thought to have originated. Crusaders discovered this rose in Damascus and brought it back to Europe when they returned home.

Moss refers to the fragrant, glaucous, mosslike growth that covers the buds, pedicels (flower stalks), sometimes the petioles (leafstalks), and even the leaflets of these curious roses.

'**Paul Neyron**' is a hybrid perpetual rose with blooms as large as 10 in. across. This plant is also remarkably disease resistant.

'**Blush Noisette**' has extremely fragrant blooms that liberally coat its 12-ft. canes from midsummer until frost.

▲ **'Moonstone'** is a hybrid tea with the typical high center. These elegant roses cut beautifully.

◀ **'China Doll'** is a polyantha that begins blooming late in the season but continues until frost.

Modern Roses

The ARS defines eight major classes of Modern Roses: floribundas, grandifloras, hybrid teas, large-flowered climbers, miniatures, polyanthas, ramblers, and shrubs. Five of these classes—the floribundas, grandifloras, hybrid teas, miniatures, and polyanthas—are subdivided into climbing and nonclimbing types.

A grower named Henry Bennett is generally considered the first person to hybridize hybrid teas and polyanthas. Hybrid teas are a cross between hybrid perpetuals and tea roses, while polyanthas resulted from a cross of *R. multiflora* and a dwarf *R. chinensis*.

In 1954, an Amerian grower crossed a hybrid tea and a floribunda to get 'Queen Elizabeth', a rose considered the first grandiflora by Americans but a floribunda by the rest of the world.

The shrub rose class includes 12 subclasses, plus one for plants that can only be classified as miscellaneous shrubs, a category that currently includes, among others,

almost all of the increasingly popular shrub-type roses developed during the last 30 or 40 years.

Roses assigned to ten of these subclasses are relatively obscure and limited in number, but the other two subclasses, the hybrid rugosas and the hybrid musks, include the best-known and most popular of the older types of shrub roses.

Classifying new roses. The genealogy of roses has become so complex, and the differences between varieties are so great that rose societies have had an increasingly difficult job of classifying newly developed cultivars. For one thing, many new hybrids don't readily fit into any of the present classes. So to eliminate the need (and the temptation) to add another new rose class to the list every few years, the ARS defined what might be called a catch-all class for climbing roses that don't fit neatly into one of the preexisting classes. As a result, roses that would have been designated as climbing hybrid teas, climbing floribundas, or climbing grandifloras just a few years ago are now classed as "large-flowered climbers."

For the same reasons, the ARS grouped together 12 "shrubby" types of roses, plus a miscellaneous category, under the general label of "shrub roses."

'Jeanne Lajoie' a miniature rose having 8-ft. canes, climbs a trellis or drapes over walls.

▲ *'Ballerina' is classified as a hybrid musk by the ARS and as a recurrent bush by the WFRS.*

◄ *'Blaze' is classified as a climbing rose by both the WFRS and the ARS.*

World Federation of Rose Societies Classifications

Outside of North America, officials of the WFRS have taken a different tact to classify roses. They've retained the definitions of Old Garden Roses and Modern Roses as well as the 15 classes of Old Garden Roses. But for the Modern Roses, they've now abandoned labels such as hybrid tea, floribunda, and hybrid musk. They have also designated a third major class—wild roses—that includes all of the species roses.

Since the WFRS adopted this international rose classification system in 1967, gardeners outside of North America have classed modern roses according to their horticultural and garden characteristics, rather than by their ancestry.

This system is very straightforward. It divides roses into climbing and nonclimbing types and separates these groups into once-flowering (nonrecurrent) and repeat-flowering (recurrent) categories. Beyond that, the WFRS describes a rose as a shrub, bush, ground cover, rambler, or miniature. The bush class includes the polyanthas and all those roses that are known in North America as hybrid teas or floribundas.

Useful Knowledge

You certainly don't need to know much about rose classes to enjoy your rose plants. However, your ability to select appropriate plants and care for them once you get them home is dramatically improved if you know the characteristics and requirements of the major classes. The roses within a class have similar cultural needs and uses in the landscape and garden. So once you know what to expect from a hybrid tea, for example, and what it looks like, you can be reasonably certain that other hybrid teas will have the same overall characteristics and cultural requirements. Most old tea roses have characteristics in common, and the same can be said for the floribundas, the noisettes, the hybrid musks, and so forth.

Of course there are outstanding exceptions in every case. It's these exceptions that make the classification systems difficult to manage, imperfect, and confusing to gardeners and experts alike.

CHAPTER TWO

Healthy Garden Soil

*R*oses, like other garden or landscape plants, need healthy and nutritious soil. But few native soils have the proper balance of nutrients without some modification. Because plants remove nutrients from the soil, and even more nutrients are flushed out by irrigation and by rainwater, you need to maintain soil to keep it in the proper condition. This is your most important garden task. To do this efficiently, you need to understand the makeup of healthy and nutritious soil, the effect of pH, and something about the biological processes within the soil.

▲ *'Floral Carpet'*
◀ ***Roses need beds*** *of well-drained sandy clay-loam soil with a pH between 6.5 to 7.5 (slightly acidic to slightly alkaline).*

Bowls containing clay, humus, loam, and sand, *clockwise from top left. It's easy to see why clay is such a poor growing medium.*

This is why clay-based soils generally drain poorly unless the gardener opens up the pore system within the soil by adding organic matter.

Clay holds too much water. Clay soils represent one extreme with respect to drainage characteristics. When they dry out, they're difficult to remoisten. When it rains or when water is sprinkled onto dry clay soil, the clay at the surface swells and plugs up the pore system. And much of the water simply runs off, having penetrated only the top inch or so.

On the other hand, if a clay soil is moistened deeply by slow soaking or by an extended period of rainy weather, it tends to hold that moisture. But because of the extremely small dimensions of the pore system, no space is left for air, and the plants drown.

Components of the Soil

Soil types range from pure sand to pure clay, with every combination in between. But all healthy soils consist of about one-half solid materials and one-half pore space. The solids consist of 90 to 95 percent rock minerals and 5 to 10 percent organic matter, mostly in the form of humus, which is decayed plant matter. And the pore space is filled with nearly equal amounts of air and water.

Sand, Silt, and Clay

Rock minerals include different-size particles—sand, silt, and clay. Individual sand and silt particles are large enough to see with the naked eye; clay particles are not. When abundant, clay particles fill the pores between the silt and sand particles, impeding the movement of water.

Sand cannot retain water. At the other extreme of drainage problems, soil that contains too much sand cannot hold water at all. Plants growing in sandy soil suffer from both malnutrition and thirst.

A healthy soil is ideally some sort of loam; that is, it contains a mixture of particle sizes. It has enough sand and silt to drain well, even though these particles contribute little or no nutrients for the plants. And it does not contain so much clay as to prevent good drainage, even though clay is the mineral component that contributes and holds plant nutrients in the soil.

Soil with a small variety of particle sizes can still be an excellent garden soil, provided that it contains enough organic matter and has a suitable pH.

An Experiment to Identify Soil Type

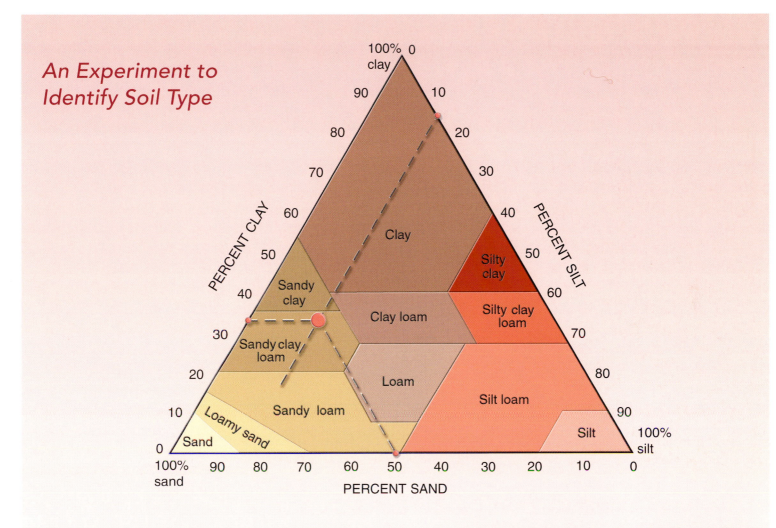

You can easily determine the type of soil you have if you know the fractional amounts of sand, silt, and clay that it contains. To find out, just fill a glass container (a fruit jar or a baby's bottle, for example) about two-thirds full of water. Then add enough dry, crumbled (no clods or lumps) soil to almost fill the container. Shake the mixture vigorously for several minutes; then set it aside. Let it rest undisturbed for a day or two or until all the solids have settled.

You'll see that the mineral particles have separated according to size. Clay (and any organic matter) will be at the top, silt will be in the middle, and sand will have settled to the bottom. With a ruler (or with the built-in scale on the baby's bottle) you can determine the approximate percentages of sand, silt, and clay in your soil. To identify the type of soil in your garden, check these amounts against the soil triangle, shown above.

For example, if your test shows 60 percent sand, 25 percent silt, and 15 percent clay, your soil is a sandy loam. But if your test indicates 50 percent sand, 15 percent silt, and 35 percent clay, you have a sandy clay loam.

Soil Drainage and Bed Preparation

To obtain more specific information about the soil where you intend to plant roses, do a percolation, or *perc*, test. Prepare your new rose bed by first outlining the area and then completely removing any turf grass or other vegetation growing.

Perc tests are an easy way to measure how well your soil drains. Use a previously dug planting hole, or dig a new hole the size and shape of a 2-pound coffee can. Fill the hole with water, and let it drain. Then fill it again, and time how long it takes for the water to drain out completely the second time.

If the water is gone in an hour or less, your soil has excellent drainage. If it requires from one to four hours, it has adequate drainage. But, if it takes more than four hours, your soil may have a drainage problem.

Hardpan may be the culprit. To investigate this further, dig or drill down a foot or so below the bottom of the test hole, and check for a layer of hardpan that might be blocking the drainage. If you find one, try to break it up mechanically; then repeat your perc test to see whether your drainage is satisfactory.

Soils with drainage problems act like buried tubs from which water does not flow out. And roses do not like wet feet. You may be able to solve your drainage problems by breaking up and amending the soil over a larger area. Or you may have to construct a raised or mounded bed, or plant the roses in containers. (See page 32 for potting mixes suited for growing roses in containers.)

Amend the soil. If the soil in your new rose bed drains adequately, till or dig the soil to a depth of at least 1 foot. Thoroughly mix in 6 to 8 inches of compost, and 4 cups of alfalfa meal for each 100 square feet of bed area. If previous soil tests have shown low magnesium or iron, add 2 cups of Epsom salts and 2 cups of iron sulfate.

Wait two or three months until the amended soil has had some time to mellow; then do a complete soil test. With the results in hand, you can make any necessary adjustments to the pH and at the same time add any other needed nutrients.

Preparing a Planting Area

DIFFICULTY LEVEL: EASY

TOOLS AND MATERIALS: Shovel, hose or watering can, finished compost, alfalfa meal, metal rake

1 **To conduct a perc test,** strip away any grass or weeds. Then dig a hole the size and shape of a 2-lb. coffee can.

2 **Fill the hole with water** and let it drain out. Fill the hole again, and keep track of how long it takes to drain a second time.

3 **Average soil drains** in 1 to 4 hrs. Dig down at least 1 ft., and mix in 8 in. of compost and 4 cups of alfalfa meal per 100 sq. ft.

4 **Smooth the area** with a metal rake, removing any dirt clods or rocks. Allow the soil to rest for two months after amending.

Soil Testing

Dig an 8-in.-deep hole, *and slice a ½-in. slab from the wall of the hole. Bag the sample.*

How to take a soil sample. Scrape or brush away any mulch or other debris from the surface. Then dig a cylindrical hole 6 to 8 inches wide and 8 to 10 inches deep. With a hand trowel, carefully slice a vertical slab, ½ inch thick, from the wall at one side of the hole, and trim the vertical edges of this slab to leave a ribbon about 2 inches wide. Put the slice of soil into a plastic bag. Repeat this process in two or three areas in the bed to get an average sample. Seal the slices of soil, crumbled and mixed together in a plastic bag, and mail it to the lab. Remember to identify from which part of your garden the sample was taken.

Where Should You Have Your Soil Tested?

Commercial laboratories, universities, and state agricultural agencies all do soil tests. Costs per sample for tests done by noncommercial laboratories range from as little as $5 to as much as $30 or $35. (And tests are offered at no cost in some areas.) Commercial laboratories typically charge from $25 to $60 or more per sample.

Even the simplest soil tests usually include four key nutrients — phosphorus, potassium, calcium, and magnesium. Available nitrogen may also be included along with the soil pH and a recommendation of the amount of limestone or sulfur needed to adjust it to a more favorable level.

A Word about Nitrogen

The quantity of available nitrogen, sometimes reported as "nitrate nitrogen," varies widely during the year because it is directly related to the biological activity in the soil. At temperatures below 50°F, soil bacteria are essentially dormant. They begin to wake up at about 60°F, but they don't become fully active until the soil reaches 70°F. As your soil warms up in the spring, you can expect to see an increasing nitrogen concentration in soil tests until the nitrogen content reaches a maximum at a soil temperature of about 85°F.

If the soil reaches 100°F, the microbial action will cease, and the nitrogen concentration will level off and begin to decline, only to rise again with the cooler temperatures of late summer and fall. Of course, a thick layer of mulch helps to lower the midsummer soil temperatures, keeping both the bacterial activity and the nitrogen concentration near the maximum.

Soil pH Scale

This table shows the availability of plant nutrients. The narrower the band width, the less available the nutrients.

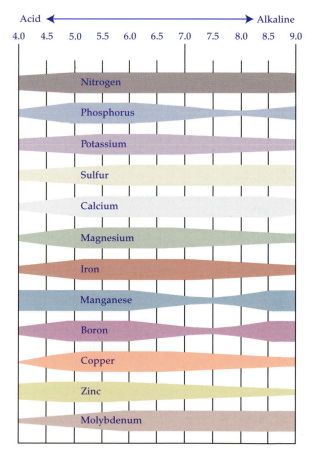

Other factors. Although this information about the available nitrogen is valuable, you must consider many other factors, such as the amounts of other macronutrients and micronutrients and the amount of organic matter necessary to maintain healthy soil.

Begin by obtaining a full-fledged, comprehensive soil test, which, regardless of the cost, is worth every dollar you spend. Be sure to specify that you want the lab to measure the soil organic matter. It will cost more, and may not be available at every lab, but it is money well spent. After you've established a baseline measure, you can get a more abbreviated soil test done every two or three years.

Measuring and Adjusting Soil pH

DIFFICULTY LEVEL: EASY

TOOLS AND MATERIALS: Trowel, probe pH meter or at-home pH test kit, gloves, bucket, lime, garden fork

1 *Probe pH meters* are a quick and easy way to measure the soil pH in the spot where you want to plant roses.

2 *Do-it-yourself pH testing kits* are adequate after a base measure is established, but they do not factor in regional soil differences.

3 *Add lime* if the pH test indicates your soil is too acid. Roses grow best with a soil pH between 6.5 and 7.5.

4 *Use a garden fork* to thoroughly mix in lime. Work the lime in several inches. Do not leave it on the soil surface.

Do-it-yourself tests. Some probe-type pH meters, sold at garden centers for about $20, do an adequate job of monitoring the pH once you've established a baseline with a formal test. The less-expensive pH test kit (shown in Step 2 on page 28), involves adding solution to a vial of soil and matching its color to a chart.

Optimal pH conditions for roses. Roses grow best in any soil with pH from 6.5 to 7.5, slightly acidic to slightly alkaline. Nutrients are sufficiently available at these levels. Roses do well enough with a pH as low as 6.0. But, if the pH is outside of that range, you need to make adjustments.

The Soil-Test Report

For acidic soils with a pH less than 6.0 or 6.5, the standard recommendation is to add limestone (calcium carbonate) or dolomite (calcium magnesium carbonate). Limestone is preferred if the soil contains sufficient magnesium, but dolomite is preferable if your soil has a magnesium deficiency. A soil-test report usually shows the appropriate rock mineral and the necessary amount. But if it doesn't, remember that 5 pounds of limestone or dolomite per 100 square feet of soil area usually raises the pH by approximately one full number. If the original pH is below 5.5, add up to 10 pounds per 100 square feet, but make the treatment in two steps a year apart.

For an alkaline soil with a pH greater than 7.5, 2 pounds of sulfur per 100 square feet will usually reduce the pH by about one full number. But add no more than 2 pounds per treatment. Also, sulfur requires biological action and up to six months to become completely effective, and that effect is only temporary.

Humus and humic acids are a more permanent solution for alkaline soils. Sufficient organic matter added to moderately alkaline soils reduces the pH to a level well within the optimal range. Remember, though, that this can require three or four years.

Organic matter. A measurement of the quantity of organic matter in the soil often costs extra and is available only by request. It is normally reported as a percentage. But

it can be either one or both of two possible measurements—either the total organic matter or only that portion of the organic matter with a particle size less than that of large sand grains (2 millimeters). The latter measurement is more significant. And for that portion of the organic matter, a concentration of only 2 or 3 percent is adequate for most soils.

Understanding Soil-Test Results

The soil-test report may include fertilizer recommendations based specifically on the nutrients in the soil and the plants you want to grow—roses, in this case. Follow

Organic fertilizers *are compost-based blends of these ingredients. You can purchase them separately in conveniently-sized bags and mix your own custom fertilizers.*

these recommendations. Scan the results for nutrients that are present in high or excess quantities. Be careful not to use any mineral or organic fertilizers containing significant amounts of those elements.

Plan your fertilizer program, synthetic or organic, so as to add larger amounts of those nutrient elements that are present in your soil only in low, inadequate concentrations.

Fertilizers and Other Additives

Now that a soil test has established which nutrients you need to add to your soil, you must select fertilizers to provide the nutrients. And there is a mind-boggling array from which you can choose. Of course, the soil-test report may include recommendations, and you can simply follow those. But even those recommendations may leave you with choices to make.

Some soil-test laboratories recommend only relatively fast-acting, synthetic fertilizers, while others recommend only fertilizers termed organic. But more and more laboratories now provide both synthetic and organic recommendations.

Using organic materials — supplemented, perhaps, by one or two slow-acting, natural mineral fertilizers — pays off in the long run. They play a large role in maintaining the health of the soil and of all its microscopic life forms.

You can often supply your roses with all of the nutrients they need while keeping a healthy balance of elements within the soil simply by adding finished compost. Otherwise, a whole suite of organic materials provides even larger concentrations of nutrients that are in short supply according to your soil-test report.

By law, fertilizer bags must list the percentages of nitrogen, phosphorus, and potassium contained in the blend.

Typical N-P-K Content of Organic Materials

Material	Nitrogen	Phosphorus	Potassium	Comments
Alfalfa Meal	4.00	1.00	2.00	Growth hormone
Bat Guano	10.00	3.00	1.00	Can burn plants
Blood Meal	15.00	1.30	0.70	Can burn plants
Coffee Grounds	2.08	0.32	0.28	Acidifying
Cottonseed Meal	7.00	2.50	1.50	Acidifying
Eggshells	1.19	0.38	0.14	High in calcium
Feather Meal	12.00	-----	-----	Can burn plants
Fish Emulsion	4.00	1.00	1.00	
Fish Meal	5.00	3.00	3.00	
Hoof and Horn Meal	12.00	2.00	0.00	Can burn plants
Human Hair	14.00	-----	-----	Can burn plants
Manure (Fresh)				
Cattle	0.29	0.17	0.10	High salt content
Chicken	1.63	1.54	0.85	High in calcium
Horse	0.44	0.17	0.35	
Rabbit	7.00	2.40	0.60	
Sheep	0.55	0.31	0.15	
Swine	0.60	0.41	0.13	
Seaweed or Kelp Meal	1.50	0.50	2.50	
Tea Grounds	4.15	0.62	0.40	
Wood Ashes				
(Leached)	-----	1.20	2.00	Highly alkaline
(Unleached)	-----	1.50	8.00	Highly alkaline
Worm Castings	0.50	0.50	0.30	Trace elements

Notes: Dried manures contain as much as five times the concentrations of the fresh products.

Materials with less than 1½ percent nitrogen will rob the soil of nitrogen as they decompose. Add a high nitrogen product to hasten decomposition and prevent temporary nitrogen depletion.

(Reprinted with permission from the Rodale Institute and the Texas Agricultural Extension Service)

Organic Fertilizers

Many brands of organic fertilizers are sold at garden centers and nurseries. Each carries a label stating its N-P-K content, such as 6-2-4, 12-4-8, 4-6-4, or 3-1-5, just to mention a few common types. And some labels also list the various organic materials included in the product.

Whenever possible, choose your fertilizer according to the needs of your soil for nitrogen, phosphorus, and potassium, as indicated by your soil-test report. Lacking that kind of information, you should choose a fertilizer for your roses with an N-P-K ratio that is a multiple of three or four parts nitrogen, one part phosphorus, and two parts potassium, such as 12-4-8.

You can also add specific organic materials — or even mix your own fertilizer blend — to provide a desired combination of nutrient elements. Beware of a couple of things, though. Whenever you add a material, such as hay, tree leaves, or eggshells, containing less than 1½ percent nitrogen, add a high-nitrogen material such as cottonseed or feather meal to offset it. Otherwise, the microbes draw too much nitrogen from the soil as they digest the low-nitrogen material, causing a temporary nitrogen shortage for your roses.

Natural Mineral Supplements

Some naturally occurring minerals are used as fertilizers to provide needed elements. Generally, these are added to sandy soils with a high silica content because these soils are often lacking in the metallic elements — calcium, magnesium, iron, and manganese. But even some clay soils are almost devoid of one or more of these necessary nutrients. Only a soil test can determine this for certain. It's never a good idea to add any nutrient just because someone else believes it's a good product and has said that it makes roses bloom better. Your soil may not have the same requirements. Once more, just because a little is good, a lot more is not necessarily better.

Gypsum is a naturally occurring mineral that is found in several different forms. It's added to sodium-based clays to make them more granular, to correct an excess of magnesium, and to alleviate a calcium deficiency. But, contrary to what some believe, gypsum does not alter the pH of the soil. However, soil bacteria act upon the sulfur and feed some of it to your plants. Gypsum is usually applied at a rate of from 2 to 4 pounds per 100 square feet, but it should never be used with soils already having an excess of calcium.

Rock Phosphate is mined at several locations around the country, and it's sold in two forms: rock phosphate and colloidal rock phosphate. Rock phosphate consists of about one-third total phosphorus (of which only about 10 to 20 percent is actually available at any one time); one-third calcium; and one-third chlorine, fluorine, and several other trace elements. Colloidal rock phosphate is a clay-size material washed out as the rock phosphate is mined. It contains only about half as much phosphorous as rock phosphate.

Apply either of these powders within the plant root zones at a rate of up to 5 pounds per 100 square feet to increase the phosphorus content of an acidic soil. Both rock and colloidal phosphates are ineffective in soil with a pH higher than 6.4. Don't use either one in soil containing an excess of calcium.

Epsom Salts, almost-pure magnesium sulfate, are a quick source of magnesium, and can also be used to make excess calcium and potassium unavailable to plants. Work one or two teaspoons into the soil around each plant, or dissolve that amount into a gallon of water and drench the plant. As a soil amendment, use no more than 1 pound per 100 square feet.

Greensand is any sedimentary material — sand, silt, or clay — that contains significant amounts of glauconite, which is a potassium iron silicate mineral. The two best-known commercial products, New Jersey greensand and Texas greensand, contain as much as 10 percent potash potassium and up to 20 percent iron. Unfortunately, most of that is not readily available to plants. Nevertheless, for many years, greensand has been used as a slow-acting potassium fertilizer for home gardens. Use at a rate of up to 5 pounds per 100 square feet.

Sul-Po-Mag, also sold as K-Mag, is a powdered form of the mineral langbeinite. This is a a form of potassium magnesium sulfate. Sul-Po-Mag contains about 22 percent soluble potash, 11 percent magnesium, and 22 percent sulfur. Do not use this supplement at rates greater than 1 pound per 100 square feet. You must be careful where and how you apply it, and it should be thoroughly watered in because it is fast-acting and can burn plants. Sul-Po-Mag also lowers the pH, which may or may not be what you want or need. It's a good idea to take a second pH reading after adding any fertilizer, but wait until it has settled.

Containers are a good option if your soil is unsuited to growing roses. The miniature rose 'Isabel Hit' is quite ornamental in these terra-cotta pots.

Be careful when adding any material with a large concentration of nitrogen. Don't apply nitrogen-rich fertilizer near your plants. Instead, scatter it around and water it in well. When soil microbes digest feather meal or bat guano, for example, they can actually generate enough heat to burn plant roots.

Clay soils can present additional problems. Excessive concentrations of phosphorus can build up when high-phosphorus fertilizers (Super Phosphate, for example) are used routinely. Such an excess can persist for years because phosphorus is essentially immobile and doesn't leach readily from a clay soil. Don't use any type of manure to fertilize a clay soil more frequently than once every three or four years. Alkaline clay soils, particularly, build up toxic levels of salts with the too-frequent application of manures, especially cattle and horse manures.

Raised beds. If your test results indicate that the soil where you plan to grow your roses has poor drainage or is completely out of balance, it may be easier to grow them in raised beds or containers.

Raised beds need to be at least 6 to 10 inches deep. Bring in 4 to 6 inches of native soil or commercial topsoil, and mix that with 3 or 4 inches of compost. Prepared planting mixes are sold for this very purpose.

You can contain your raised bed within a retaining wall constructed of almost any landscaping material of your choice, including wooden timbers, concrete blocks, bricks, rocks, or plastic barriers of various designs. Or you can simply rake the sides of the bed at a 45-degree angle. An amended, well-mulched soil usually stays in place well enough without any solid retaining wall.

Container Soil. For container gardening, use a bagged organic potting soil obtained at the garden center. Many good-quality brands are available, so ask local gardeners which one they recommend for roses. Or, if you prefer, you can mix your own potting soil, using any one of several popular approaches and formulas. Stay away from peat moss, which is too acidic, hard to moisten, and dries out too quickly in an outdoor environment.

Smart Tip
Peat-less Potting Soils

Here are three peat-less formulas for potting soils that you can mix yourself, using only bagged or packaged products available at many nurseries and garden centers.

Simple Shrub Mix: *Yield: 12 quarts*
8 quarts coarse-screened compost
4 quarts sharp sand
2 cups composted manure
1 cup alfalfa meal
¼ cup each rock phosphate and gypsum

Soilless mix: *Yield: 17 quarts*
8 quarts coarse-screened compost
8 quarts vermiculite
1 quart composted manure
1 cup cottonseed meal
1½ tablespoons each rock phosphate and gypsum

Compost-Soil Mix: *Yield: 19 quarts*
4 quarts vermiculite
4 quarts perlite
6 quarts good quality, bagged topsoil
4 quarts compost
1 quart composted manure
1 cup each rock phosphate and gypsum

Plant Nutrients

Plants are composed mostly of carbon (C), hydrogen (H) and oxygen (O), three chemical elements obtained directly from the air, from carbon dioxide, and from water. But scientists have identified at least 14 additional elements that are essential for normal plant growth.

Six of these, calcium (Ca), magnesium (Mg), nitrogen (N), phosphorus (P), potassium (K), and sulfur (S) are categorized as macronutrients because plants require them in comparatively large amounts. Except for a portion of the nitrogen, all these macronutrients are obtained from soil solids, mostly with the aid of bacteria and other microorganisms.

It's helpful to remember these major nutrients, because these nine, plus iron (Fe), are the elements most likely to be included in soil analyses and listed on bags of fertilizer. One easy way to remember them is to become acquainted with that noted hash house honcho:

C. HOPK(i)NS, CaFe Mg(r)

decoded, from left to right, as carbon, hydrogen, oxygen, phosphorus, potassium, nitrogen, sulfur, calcium, iron, and magnesium.

The remaining eight essential elements are categorized as micronutrients, or trace elements, not because they're smaller or less essential to plant growth, but because they're required in small amounts. These elements are boron (B), chlorine (Cl), cobalt (Co), copper (Cu), iron (Fe), manganese (Mn), molybdenum (Mo), and zinc (Zn), all of which are obtained from soil solids. Soil tests determine the status of each of the important nutrient elements — both the deficiencies and the excesses.

Concentrations of nutrient elements may be reported only in relative terms, such as *low, medium,* and *high*. But they are more commonly reported in quantitative terms

Chlorosis is an iron deficiency, which causes younger rose leaves to turn yellow, while the veins remain green.

A magnesium deficiency is evident on this rose leaf.

as *parts per million* (ppm) or *pounds per acre*. Of course, specific numbers are subject to more precise interpretation than are the general descriptions of low, medium, or high. The chart below relates the numbers to the more general terms.

Rating	P ppm	K ppm	Ca ppm	Mg ppm
Very Low	0 – 5	0 – 90		
Low	6 – 10	91 – 130	0 – 250	0 – 50
Medium	11 – 20	131 – 175	251 – 750	51 – 150
High	21 – 40	176 – 300	751 – 2000	> 150
Very High	> 40	> 300	> 2000	

According to standards accepted by the agricultural industry, 1 acre of soil, 6 inches deep (a furrow or plow slice), has a weight of approximately 2 million pounds. You need only to multiply measurements expressed in parts per million by a factor of two to obtain their equivalents in pounds per acre. For example, a concentration of 16 parts per million is equivalent to 32 pounds per acre. And, 480 pounds per acre corresponds to 240 parts per million.

Microbes — Those Critters in the Soil

When organic gardeners advise us to feed the soil rather than the plants, they mean that we should feed the microorganisms in the soil. That's just common sense because the microbes that nourish our plants depend on us for much of their food. But the living plants also do their part. Roots break up the soil and remove moisture. As roots decompose, they provide building materials for humus.

Organic acids formed at the root surfaces dissolve minerals, thereby releasing nutrients to help replace those absorbed by the plants. And excretion of amino acids by decaying organic matter and soil microbes, along with sloughing of root tissues, further stimulates the action of microorganisms.

Nematodes

A beneficial nematode investigating a mite

On the average, about 2,800 nematodes inhabit every ounce (two tablespoons) of garden soil, and the most numerous of those are beneficial. They live on decaying organic matter or prey on other nematodes and on bacteria, algae, and protozoa. The least numerous, but the ones rightfully dreaded by gardeners, are root-knot nema-todes, the parasites that live on or in plant roots, especially vegetable roots, but not excluding roses.

Protozoa

A colony of protozoa under a microscope

Protozoa are the most varied and, at about 2.8 million per ounce of soil, the most numerous of the microfauna. They ingest bacteria and, to a lesser extent, some algae and fungi. Some protozoa are quite rugged and can withstand temperatures of at least 120°F and an acidic pH as low as 2.0.

Algae

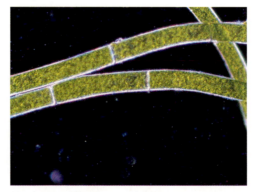

Freshwater filamentous algae

Most types of algae live at or near the surface because they're chlorophyll-bearing organisms capable of photosynthesis. But a few forms obtain their energy from organic

Euglena algae (color enhanced)

matter and live deeper in the soil. All algae, which can number 2.8 million per ounce of soil, are stimulated by manures.

Fungi

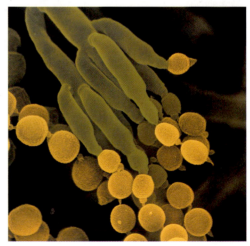

Penicillin fungus (Penicillium chrysogenum)

Fungi can't produce chlorophyll, so they depend on organic matter for energy and carbon. An ounce of fertile soil will contain about 28 million of three types: yeasts, molds, and mushroom fungi. Most molds are found near the surface, where they're the most versatile and persistent of all the soil microorganisms. Some of the almost-microscopic mushroom fungi form a symbi-otic relationship with plant roots known as mycorrhizae, or "fungus root." This association increases the uptake of plant nutrients, notably phosphorus. In return, the fungi receive carbohydrates from the plant.

Actinomycetes

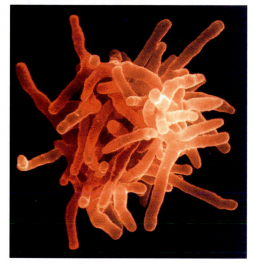

Actinomycetes *bacteria*

Actinomycetes remain more active during droughts than the true bacteria and the molds, but they thrive in moist, well-aerated soils with a pH between 6.0 and 7.5. They don't do well in acidic conditions and disappear almost entirely if the soil pH drops below 5.0.

When stimulated by manures, the numbers of actinomycetes can grow to 2.8 billion per ounce of soil. Only the true bacteria are more numerous. Hence, they're of great importance in the decomposition of organic matter and for the liberation of plant nutrients. And they have a special capability for breaking down more resistant compounds, such as *cellulose, chitin,* and *phospholipids* (a primary organic source of phosphorus). They're also the critters responsible for the sweet aroma of freshly turned earth.

Bacteria

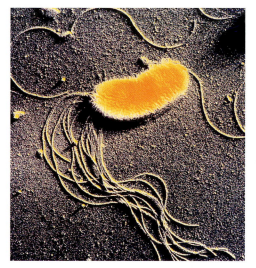

Soil bacteria

Bacteria are the most populous and arguably the most important soil microorganisms of all, and an ounce of healthy garden soil contains about 28 billion individuals of several types. Bacteria are most populous near the surface because of favorable temperature, moisture, aeration and food conditions. Bacteria prefer about the same moisture level as do most plants.

Some bacteria function in very acidic conditions, and some at a very high pH, but most prefer a pH between 6.0 and 8.0,

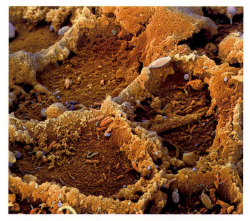

Bacteria on a partially decomposed leaf

provided that the soil is rich in calcium. In fact, there's some evidence that the quantity of calcium is more important than the pH. As a group, bacteria are responsible for nitrogen fixation, for the formation of nitrates and sulfur oxidation. Hence, they rival or surpass both fungi and actinomycetes in performing the vital processes in the soil.

So, feed your soil, and you'll help feed all those little critters—all the nematodes, protozoa, algae, fungi, actinomycetes, and bacteria—that feed your plants.

Earthworms

Earthworms in a handful of soil

Earthworms consume and process both organic matter and minerals in the soil, subjecting them to digestive enzymes and breaking them down chemically. Consequently, excreted earthworm castings have high concentrations of bacteria and of calcium, magnesium, phosphorus, potassium, nitrate nitrogen, and partially processed organic matter. Earthworms bring deeper soil minerals to the surface and take organic matter back down, stirring and aerating the soil with their burrows as they go. Significant numbers of earthworms indicate a healthy and nutritious soil. They should be cherished and treated with respect by every gardener.

Composting Wastes

Finished compost is essential for healthy soil and is an excellent mulch.

Finished compost is absolutely the best soil amendment for all types of soils—and it's excellent to use for mulch. But you may need a large amount of compost to maintain good, fertile soil. And that much compost, whether you purchase it by the bag or by the pickup-truck load, is often difficult to locate or prohibitively expensive.

The good news is that compost is easy to make yourself and so valuable that every gardener can and should compost. You can do it as elaborately or as simply as your space, budget, and desire for exercise allow. After all, as someone once said, "There are only three steps to successful composting: First gather up all the grass, leaves, and green garbage you can find; pile it up somewhere; and let it rot. Everything else is just gilding the lily."

For example, 1 cubic yard or more of an optimal mixture of shredded "brown" and "green" material, remixed thoroughly every three or four days, can result in a half cubic yard of sweet-smelling, finished compost in as little as two or three weeks.

The Mixture

Fundamentally, composting is nothing more than the digestion of organic matter by microbes. They function best with a balanced diet consisting of about 30 parts of fuel or energy (brown stuff, carbohydrates, or carbon) for every 1 part of the stuff needed to grow and reproduce (green stuff, proteins or nitrogen). This 30:1 ratio of

"browns" to "greens" is considered ideal for composting, and one that you should always try to approximate.

Grass clippings and tree leaves are the two materials most commonly available for a compost pile. Grass clippings are essentially green stuff and high in nitrogen, and tree leaves are brown stuff and high in carbon. One bag of shredded tree leaves can be mixed with two bags of grass clippings to result in a carbon/nitrogen ratio of approximately 32:1, or very near the ideal mixture.

But tree leaves are mostly available in the fall, and grass clippings are available only during mowing season. This doesn't have to be a concern. Gather the leaves, and save them over the winter in a pile or in plastic bags. Then shred them and add them to the compost pile whenever you add grass clippings.

You can also use other types of organic matter in your compost pile, including vegetable waste from the kitchen, shredded paper, and rotted manure. Each of

Carbon-to-Nitrogen Ratios For the Compost Heap

Corn Stalks	60:1
Fruit Waste	35:1
Grass Clippings	9:1
Hay:	
Alfalfa	12:1
Legume, grass	25:1
Kitchen Vegetable Waste	15:1
Oat Straw	80:1
Paper	170:1
Rotted Manure	20:1
Sawdust	500:1
Straw	80:1
Sugar Cane Residue	60:1
Tree Leaves	60:1
Wood Shavings	700:1

these has its own carbon-to-nitrogen ratio and should be used only in amounts that will maintain an overall ratio of approximately 30:1. (See the table at left.)

Some people add an inoculant, such as fresh manure or garden soil, to initiate the biological activity. But there's already an adequate supply of microbes in any kind of plant waste.

What not to compost. Some items should not be added to most compost piles, even though they decompose along with everything else. These include meat scraps and fatty wastes, cat and dog feces, and diseased plant materials. Meat scraps and fatty wastes attract dogs, cats, raccoons, and rodents. Do not compost cat and dog feces because they may carry dangerous viruses. Rabbit droppings and farm animal manure are entirely acceptable in a compost pile.

Sustained temperatures of 170°F are necessary to destroy plant pathogens and weed seeds. But, while a truly active compost pile can get this hot, sustained temperatures of 140°F to 150°F are more likely.

In any case, no obtainable composting temperature can kill either viruses or botrytis fungi. Ultimately, you alone can decide about adding other diseased plants. If you can keep the temperature at 160°F for at least 48 to 72 hours, it's probably safe to include them. Otherwise, leave them out.

To Contain or Not to Contain

You can be successful at composting by just heaping all the materials in a pile somewhere. But most people prefer to contain the pile just to keep things neat.

Rolling composters are easier but produce less. If you prefer not having to turn your pile with a garden fork or mattock, purchase a rolling barrel or hand-cranked tumbler sold by garden centers and mail-order gardening supply firms. The choice is entirely up to you; they all do the job. But even though barrels and tumblers may require less labor on your part, only an open-air pile can be used to make more than just a minimum amount of compost.

Garden and kitchen-waste materials are the raw ingredients for compost. Try to maintain a balance of 30:1 carbon to nitrogen as you build the pile.

Measure the temperature (and biological activity) inside your pile with a compost thermometer.

Building a Compost Pile

DIFFICULTY LEVEL: EASY

TOOLS AND MATERIALS: Gloves, wheelbarrow, garden fork, hose, wire bin, heavy black plastic, PVC pipes

1 **Use a garden fork** to grab bunches of nitrogen-rich green material, and add it to the brown matter already in the compost heap.

2 **Mist the pile** with a hose. The pile should be glistening, but not soaking wet, about as moist as a wrung-out sponge.

Building the Pile

Put only shredded materials in your compost pile. A lawn mower shreds grass clippings and leaves adequately. To pulverize leaves and small twigs, use either an electric or gasoline-powered, over-the-shoulder blower/shredder.

Start with a 3-by-3-foot heap. The composting process starts more rapidly and becomes more intense if you mix all the materials into a single pile at least 3 feet deep and leave it to cook instead of building it by layers. You can locate your pile in any convenient place. Once you assemble the pile, water it so that it's evenly damp throughout, but not saturated. Then cover it with a sheet of black plastic to retain moisture and to prevent any rainfall from flushing out any of the nutrients.

Get a compost thermometer and, after a day or two, take the pile's temperature by putting the thermometer deep into the pile. If everything is working properly, the temperature will be at least 110°F after a couple of days, and it will reach 140°F or more in three or four days. If the

3 **Cover the pile** *to retain the moisture and the heat generated by the soil organisms breaking down the raw materials.*

4 **Skewer the plastic** *on the PVC pipes to hold it in place. If you didn't used pipes, tie the plastic to the frame so it doesn't blow off.*

pile is untended, the temperature will reach 150° to 170°F and then begin to decline. This can occur in about a week.

Turning the Pile

Turning a compost pile remixes everything and presents the microbes with fresh fodder and a replenished supply of oxygen. This is especially important for the materials near the edges of the pile where temperatures don't get as hot and decomposition doesn't happen as fast as in the center of the pile. For finished compost in the shortest time, turn your pile every four or five days. Otherwise, you can wait until the temperature has fallen back to about 120°F.

"Turning" the pile is a misnomer. You want to thoroughly remix the materials. And you can accomplish this best with a heavy mattock or a garden fork. First, remove the fence or open the walls that surround the pile. Then chop down into it and spread the materials out, either with the mattock or with the fork held in a vertical posi-

Turning a Compost Pile

DIFFICULTY LEVEL: EASY

TOOLS AND MATERIALS: Wheelbarrow, garden fork, 1 cup of alfalfa meal

1 *Use a garden fork* or mattock to chop down the pile and spread the material out flat.

2 *Fork the material taken from the inside* of the pile outside the edges of the flattened pile.

tion. Once you've raked the outer materials into a new pile, heap the inside portion onto and around the material you removed from the outer edges of the pile. Don't be concerned if the outer parts of the original pile have an obvious buildup of fungus. That's normal. Fungi play an important role in the decomposition process.

You can contain the reworked pile where it stands, or you can fork it back into its original container. In any case, you've thoroughly remixed all the materials. What was on the outside is now at the center, and what was in the center is at or near the outside of the new pile. This process ensures that all of the raw materials are subject to the same hot temperatures and high microbial activities.

Monitor the temperature. Continue measuring the temperature of your pile each day. It will begin to climb toward 140°F almost immediately. After going through this cycle four or five times, note when the temperature levels off to about 110°F. The compost is ready when this occurs. The finished compost will be a uniform, dark brown color and have a delicious earthy aroma. At this stage, you'll be able to recognize only a few pieces of larger, tougher materials, and even those will be in an obvious state of decay.

Passive composting also works, but not as fast. Turn the compost pile, as described on page 39 and in the

3 **Add 1 cup of alfalfa meal** to raise the temperature of the compost pile. Alfalfa is an excellent source of nitrogen.

4 **Set up a wire frame** to contain the compost pile on its new site. Or rebuild the pile and set up the frame around it.

5 **Fork the material taken from the outside** of the pile into the bin, and put what was the inside on top.

sequence above, every five days only if you need finished compost in a rush.

If you prefer a more leisurely approach, or if your back is not up to this much work, try to rebuild your pile about three times a season. In between, be sure to keep it slightly moist.

Problems and Solutions

There aren't many things that can go seriously wrong with the composting process. If your pile doesn't heat up to at least 140°F on the first cycle, then it doesn't contain enough nitrogen-rich green stuff, and you can add more at the first turning. If you detect more than an occasional whiff of ammonia, your pile contains too much green matter. This doesn't hurt the composting process, but it does slow it down. So you might consider increasing the carbon content by mixing in sawdust or wood shavings. Just be careful not to overdo it.

Keep moisture level consistent. The only other thing that can go wrong is for the pile to dry out or become too wet. The compost should have the dampness of a wrung-out sponge at all times. Check by squeezing some of the materials in your hand each time you turn the pile. The soil organisms will operate most efficiently at this correct moisture level.

CHAPTER THREE

Selecting and Planting Roses

Once you've decided which rose cultivar you want to plant in your garden or landscape, you're immediately confronted with additional decisions. Do you want a budded rose or one growing on its own roots? Should it be bare-root or container-grown? Patented or non-patented? What grade should it be? How should it be planted?

These aren't necessarily difficult decisions, and some of them may have already been made for you. But selecting roses does take some thought. It also helps to be familiar with the terms that are used to describe roses before shopping for them by mail or in local garden centers.

▲ **'Champagne Cocktail'** *a floribunda rose*

◄ **Roses** *in this garden have been chosen as much for their ability to resist many common diseases as for their beauty.*

Own-Root and Budded Roses

Own-root and *budded* are important terms for rose growers. They describe the way the rose was propagated. Own-root roses grow on their own roots. But the top growth of a budded or grafted plant grows on the root system of an entirely different variety.

If you look down near the soil line of a container-grown budded rose or just below the canes on a budded bare-root plant, you'll see a swollen and knob-like part of the stem. The canes all originate from this spot, called the *bud union,* because this is where the grower grafted, or budded, the selected cultivar onto the rootstock.

Own-Root Roses

An own-root rose is a true clone of the original plant. It develops from cuttings taken from a mother plant. These cuttings are individually rooted, usually in a greenhouse environment under a water misting system. The grower transplants each cutting that successfully develops roots to increasingly larger containers until it's mature enough to sell, typically when it's two or three years old.

Antique roses, *such as these R. rugosa are commonly grown on their own roots. They take a little longer to develop, but they will always come true to type if their top growth is killed by freezing temperatures.*

Check the stems *of roses you are buying to see whether the plants are own-root or budded.*

Budded Roses

Creating a budded rose is a several-step process. The grower first selects a suitable rootstock and cuts T-shaped slots low on one of its canes. The next step is to cut off dormant bud eyes from a mother plant of the chosen cultivar and place one or more of them into the slots on the rootstock cane. Once the buds take hold and canes sprout from them, it's safe to cut off the top growth of the original rootstock. Growers plant budded roses in an open field and usually let them grow for two years or until they reach salable size.

Own-Root or Budded?

For commercial propagators, the choice between growing own-root or budded stock is first a matter of economics and secondly a matter of biology. Budding is far less expensive than working with cuttings. A single cutting makes only one own-root rose but may contain five or six bud eyes that could develop into other plants. Budded roses grow outside, with little care, but cuttings always require expensive greenhouse space and repotting.

Budded and Grafted

The terms *budded* and *grafted* are sometimes used as synonyms because growth buds are, in effect, grafted onto the rootstock. While rose canes can be grafted onto a rootstock in the same way that fruit and nut trees are, roses are more often budded.

Biological concerns. Some roses root so poorly from cuttings that it's best to bud them. Others, particularly some of the modern hybrids, have such weak systems that they have difficulty surviving on their own roots in a garden. Growers may also select particular rootstocks because of their resistance to pests and diseases or their suitability for a certain soil type or climate. As a result, almost all hybrid teas, floribundas, grandifloras, and large-flowered climbers are budded roses, as are many modern shrub roses. In contrast, customer demand means that most antique and other Old Garden roses are own-root plants; only the large mail-order firms offer them as budded roses on alien rootstocks. Miniature roses are always sold on their own roots, too.

Choosing Roses

When you are deciding which type of rose to choose—own-root or budded, you'll soon discover that you have several things to consider when making the decision.

Pros and Cons

Budded roses have well-developed root systems, are usually sold when they are more mature, and—with the exception of some climbing roses—begin to flower handsomely during the first year.

Own-root roses, on the other hand, are usually sold at a smaller and younger stage than budded plants. They typically require at least two or three years in the ground to fully catch up with their budded brethren in both size and performance.

Older rose species *sometimes send up new shoots each season and develop into large thickets. Growing them on a more demure rootstock prevents this spreading.*

But while most budded roses produce satisfactorily for only 5 to perhaps 15 years, own-root roses may thrive for a century or more. Remember, too, that when that inevitable, extra-cold winter comes along and the top growth of a rose freezes, only its root system may survive. In that case, roses growing on their own roots may take a while to recover, but they always come back true to form. Budded roses won't. Seemingly like magic, a strange new plant with entirely different flowers and form will appear where a cherished rose once stood.

Smart Tip
Removing Suckers

The rootstock on your budded or grafted rose may send up suckers—long bristly canes covered with leaves that are obviously not the same as those of the budded or grafted rose. Cut off these suckers at their origins, because they rob energy from the top growth.

'**Dr. Huey**' is a common rootstock because of its tolerance for alkaline soils. But you don't usually see the dark red flowers unless the top growth of one of those roses is winter-killed.

'**New Dawn**' has the honor of holding the first plant patent, issued in 1930. This pink climbing rose is still a favorite of gardeners all over the country.

standard rootstock because it's considered appropriate for acid soils and is somewhat cold hardy. In very cold climates, growers frequently use the wild dog rose of Europe, *Rosa canina,* as a standard rootstock.

Growers in the sandy soils of southern Florida use 'Fortuniana' as a rootstock for both modern and antique roses. This rose is supposedly an 1850 cross between two climbing roses, 'Lady Banks' (*Rosa banksiae*) and 'Cherokee' (*Rosa laevigata*), and is sometimes called 'Double Cherokee'. It has an extensive feeder root system and is highly resistant to the bane of South Florida gardeners, the dreaded root-knot nematode.

Every gardener who wants to grow budded roses would like to have them on a rootstock chosen specifically for the local soil and climate. But with both wholesalers and mail- order retailers shipping roses throughout the country, gardeners often have to take whatever is available. And other than for the relative cold tenderness

Smart Tip
Blooming Rootstocks

When the top growth of a rose freezes and dies, the rootstock often survives and blooms the following season, just as this *R. multiflora* has done. If your rose sports new flowers one year, suspect that the top growth has died and the rootstock has taken over.

More Rootstocks

Many roses are used as rootstocks, generally because they grow quickly and have stout canes. 'Dr. Huey' is popular in the southwest United States. Some California growers use 'Gloire des Rosomanes', also known as 'Ragged Robin', while others use the versatile 'Manetti'. 'Gloire des Rosomanes' is a repeat-blooming hybrid China rose with clusters of large, fragrant, crimson flowers, and 'Manetti' is a repeat-blooming noisette rose that bears small clusters of 2-inch, semidouble pink flowers.

Growers in the eastern part of North Ameria often use a variety of the wild Chinese rose, *Rosa multiflora*, as a of 'Fortuniana', which limits its use to somewhat warmer regions, the choice of rootstock is often academic.

Patented or Nonpatented?

Many new rose varieties are patented. Patents give the developer (or whoever owns the patent) exclusive rights to propagate that variety for a period of 17 to 20 years. Because it's an expensive process, not every new variety of rose is patented, but most nonpatented roses are simply older than 20. Unless you're planning on propagating your new rose, it makes no difference whether you buy a patented or a nonpatented variety.

Bare-Root and Container Roses

Roses are sold as either bare-root or container-grown plants. Bare-root roses are dug, packaged, shipped, and sold in a state of dormancy. They are available at the garden center and through mail-order suppliers only in late winter and early spring. Before selling them, the supplier removes the soil from their roots. Damp excelsior or sphagnum peat moss keeps them moist while they are traveling or waiting for a buyer in the store. In addition, some suppliers dip the naked canes in paraffin so that they don't become dehydrated.

Even when roses arrive at a nursery in a bare-root condition, the staff may pot them in *papier-mâché* containers before placing them on display. These plants are not container-grown roses; they are simply placed in a container before sale.

True container-grown roses are just that—they grew in a 1- to 5-gallon container and were not repotted just for sale. Container-grown roses may be purchased almost any time during the growing season.

In general, nurseries offer budded roses as bare-root plants and own-root roses as container-grown plants. However, exceptions abound. Some suppliers grow budded roses for a time in containers before selling them. You may also see own-root roses prepared and sold as bare-root plants.

◀ **Bare-root roses** *must be planted while they are still dormant.*

▶ **Container-grown** *roses transplant well at any time during the season, even when they are blooming. Set them where you will plant them, and adjust the spacing to give them adequate room.*

For the gardener, there is little difference between bare-root and container-grown roses, other than for the restrictions imposed by the time of year. Plant a bare-root rose as early in the season as possible so that it has time to become established before the heat of summer. It needs time to develop enough of a feeder-root system to supply adequate moisture and nutrients to its foliage and flowers during the stressful days of summer.

On the other hand, plant container-grown roses at any time of the year so long as the ground is unfrozen. If the plants are watered properly, this includes, in theory at least, the dog days of summer.

Choosing the Plant

Nurseries classify budded roses as Grade 1, Grade $1^1/2$, and Grade 2 plants. Grade 1 hybrid teas, floribundas, grandifloras, and large-flowered climbers have a minimum of three long, strong, and sturdy canes with at least one of them $1/2$ inch or more in diameter when measured within 3 inches of the bud union. Polyanthas have four or more mature canes of this size.

Grade $1^1/2$ roses have two or more strong and sturdy canes. When Grade 1 roses aren't available, healthy grade $1^1/2$ roses are acceptable. Grade 2 roses are bargain-counter plants; to qualify as Grade 2, the plants must have a minimum of two canes at least 12 inches long. If the plant is healthy, you can take a chance on a Grade 2 plant. It may become a fine rose—just don't count on it.

Check the canes too. Select canes of bare-root roses that are smooth and plump, with creamy white centers and no dried or discolored growth buds. Check that the root system is well-developed, sturdy, and undamaged. Minor breaks in some of the smaller roots aren't important; you'll trim off that damage. But significant damage to the main roots isn't acceptable; this is sufficient reason to return a plant for an exchange or a refund.

No numerical grading system exists for container-grown, own-root roses, but use similar criteria to judge

'Iceberg', a floribunda rose, is so popular that you are bound to find it in garden centers and nurseries all across the country.

Locating the Bud Union

—bud union

Bud unions are protected from the elements when they are set 3 in. to 6 in. below the soil surface. At this depth and with mulch, they are unlikely to die from the cold.

them. Look for sturdy, healthy, branching canes that are an appropriate size for the age of the plant; choose roses with symmetrically spaced canes. Be sure that the plant is anchored solidly in the growing medium. Lastly, look for clean and healthy foliage, with no signs of insect pests or disease damage.

Locating the Bud Union

Most rose experts advise planting budded or grafted roses so that the bud union is 3 to 6 inches below the soil surface. This anchors the rose solidly. Also, the top growth, which is the rose variety of choice, often develops its own root system from the buried canes just above the bud union. If the rose happens to be killed back to the ground during an unexpectedly cold winter, these roots make it more likely to re-sprout true to form, rather than as another 'Dr. Huey' or some other alien rootstock.

Planting Your Roses

Bare-Root Roses

Plant bare-root roses as soon as the soil can be worked in late winter or early spring, preferably not later than the average date of the last frost in your area.

Prepare the spot. Dig a hole at least 18 to 24 inches wide and 18 inches deep. If you've already prepared your soil for planting, mix 2 cups of compost or well-aged cow or cattle manure with the soil you removed from the hole. If you have not already prepared the soil, add 2 cups of cow or cattle manure and 1 cup of alfalfa meal to a mixture of two parts native soil and one part compost. Use this mixture to build the mound and backfill into the hole.

Planting Bare-Root Roses

DIFFICULTY LEVEL: EASY

TOOLS AND MATERIALS: Plastic wrap, bucket, vitamin tonic and root stimulator, and organic mulch

1 *Don't let the roots dry out. As soon as you get the rose, unwrap it, remoisten the packing material, and rewrap it in plastic if you can't plant it the next day.*

2 *Trim off any damaged rootlets, and soak the plant overnight in a bucket of water containing eight or ten drops of a vitamin tonic and root stimulator made for roses.*

3 *After forming a mound with the amended soil and packing it firmly, spread the roots over the mound. In colder climates, the bud union should be below soil level, as shown.*

4 *After watering the root area thoroughly, fill the hole with prepared soil, tamping firmly around the roots to remove any air pockets. Water the soil again thoroughly.*

5 *Mound soil 6 in. high around the plant to protect it from the elements. Over the next month, gradually pull the extra soil away; then add an organic mulch.*

Smart Tip
Heat Protection

If the temperature climbs above 85°F during the first three or four weeks after planting and before your bare-root rose has completely leafed out, erect a small canopy over the rose to provide shade during the brightest, hottest part of the day.

Planting Container-Grown Roses

Dig a hole that's about twice the diameter and half again as deep as the rose's container—but not less than 18 inches wide and 12 inches deep. Mix a cup of composted or well-aged cattle or cow manure with your prepared garden soil. If your soil is a little lean, you can augment it by combining the cup of composted or aged manure with a handful of alfalfa meal before mixing it with a mixture of one part compost and two parts of the native soil taken from the hole. Put enough of this amended soil in the hole to position the top of the container soil so that the bud union is at the correct depth.

Smart Tip
Planting Exceptions

There are two times when you should handle a container-grown rose as a bare-root plant. If the root ball disintegrates when you slip it out of the container, wash off the soil, and plant as a bare-root plant. Or if your rose is in a container that says to plant the whole thing, remove the pot, and plant the rose without it.

Planting a Rose in a Container

DIFFICULTY LEVEL: EASY

TOOLS AND MATERIALS: By-pass pruners, straight stick, shovel, and organic mulch.

1 *After watering the pot, lay it on its side, and roll it gently while pressing on the outside to loosen the roots.*

2 *If any roots are circling the container soil, cut them free, or pull them loose with your fingers.*

3 *Position the plant carefully. Use a stick across the planting hole to check that the bud union is at the desired depth.*

4 *Fill the hole with the prepared soil, working it in around the roots. Water the soil as you fill to eliminate any air pockets.*

Climbing roses thrive on freestanding fences because of the excellent air circulation on all sides.

Climbing Roses

Plant climbing roses as you do any other rose, but unless you plan to grow them as freestanding, arching shrubs, you must provide a sturdy support that allows enough air circulation around the canes to keep them healthy.

If your rose is to grow on a pillar or other type of trellis, plant it at the base of the structure, and trim and tie it in place. Tie the canes as loosely as practical, with a soft flexible material, to avoid damaging the wood and to allow room for growth. Wire or nylon cord will cut into the canes.

If your rose will climb up into a tree, plant it in between the roots and at least 18 to 24 inches away from the trunk. This allows the space for good air circulation and keeps root competition to a minimum.

Smart Tip
Training Climbers

Train climbing roses so that as many shoots as possible grow horizontally, because horizontal canes flower in many more places than do vertical shoots.

Growing Roses on Attached Trellises

DIFFICULTY LEVEL: MODERATE

TOOLS AND MATERIALS: Trellis, space boards, eye bolts, long hooks, shovel

1 *Attach the trellis with wooden spacers and long hooks to protect your plant from fungal diseases. The space allows air to circulate between the plant and any solid structure behind it.*

2 *Tie the canes to the trellis with soft cloth or twist-ties. Make a figure eight with the tie to keep it from cutting into the rose cane.*

Planting in a Container

Native soil, amended or not, is not appropriate for plants in a container. For one thing, it lacks the drainage characteristics that helps to keep plants healthy, and for another, it's unlikely to be light enough to withstand the compaction that overhead watering always creates. So instead of using a native soil, purchase a good quality organic potting soil at a garden center, or mix one yourself that is composed of two parts compost and one part each of peat moss and a vermiculite/perlite mix.

Planting. Use the same procedure to plant any rose—bare-root or container-grown, own-root or budded—in a container as you would use to plant that rose in the ground. Just think of the container as a pre-dug hole, and choose one that's large enough.

Container size requirements are most obvious when you plant a bare-root rose. You can plant in any container that is wide and deep enough so that you don't have to trim, twist, or curl the plant roots when you place them in the pot. As in the ground, let the roots drape over the cone-shaped mound that you'll construct. When planting a container-grown plant, choose a pot that is at least twice as wide as the container in which the rose is already growing.

It's neither necessary nor even a good idea to put broken pottery, pebbles, or other drainage materials in the bottom of your container. If you need something to prevent the potting soil from falling through the bottom drain holes of the pot, simply place a paper towel over them. The towel retains the soil but still lets water drain out. And microbes will compost the paper after the soil has settled into place.

Planting a Rose in a Container

DIFFICULTY LEVEL: EASY

TOOLS AND MATERIALS: Large container, potting soil, paper towels, straight stick, trowel, water

1 Place paper towels over the drain holes in the container. The towels prevent soil from falling out but don't add weight to the pot.

2 Use a good quality potting soil in the container. Add a moderate portion, and shape it into a mound before draping the roots over it.

3 Check that the rose is level and that the bud union is correctly placed by measuring it against a straight stick placed across the top of the pot.

4 Water the soil well to remove possible air holes both when the pot is half-filled and again when it is completely full.

Replacing a Rose with a Rose

DIFFICULTY LEVEL: EASY

TOOLS AND MATERIALS: Shovel, tarp or groundcloth, wheelbarrow, bagged top soil, and rose

1 *Before replacing a rose with another rose, remove all the roots and surrounding soil by digging out an area at least 30 in. wide by 18 in. deep.*

2 *Fill the hole with new soil, and amend it as usual. Plant your rose as shown on page 48. Watch it carefully, and move the rose if it doesn't thrive.*

Replacing an Existing Rose

If you decide to replace an existing rose with another rose plant, you must take certain precautions. Several experts have observed that a rose placed directly into the same soil in which another rose has grown for a couple of years or more can suffer from what has been called either "soil exhaustion" or "rose sickness." The new rose never develops into a strong and vigorous plant and may, in fact, wither and die, a fate that seems to occur most frequently and most severely in light, sandy soils.

A least three theories have been advanced to explain this phenomenon. One faction holds that rose roots excrete some sort of toxin that inhibits the growth of the roots of other roses. They say that it's important to remove all the soil that was in contact with the previous rose's roots whenever one rose is replaced with another.

A second group holds that decaying rose roots emit a poisonous toxin. They say that it's not actually necessary to replace the soil when planting the second rose, provided all of the roots of the first rose have been removed.

Yet a third group suggests that the remaining roots and root hairs of the original rose leave behind a network of tunnels as they decay. The roots of the new rose, taking the path of least resistance, grow into these tunnels, thereby failing to make proper contact with the soil and with the microbes in the soil. Or, if they do make contact, they encounter a toxin. These experts also suggest that the mycorrhizal fungi might never develop properly within the new root system. In any case, the roots never become capable of adequately sustaining the top growth.

CHAPTER FOUR

Companions for Roses

Roses thrive with companions, provided that the other plants don't hog all the space or consume too much of the food and water. For the greatest success, try growing only compatible plants—those with similar requirements that do well in the same type of soil and have the same needs for water, fertilizer, and sunlight. The best companions for roses have either shallow, noninvasive root systems or a single, deep taproot. This chapter takes a look at the best companion plants, plus some plants that do not make good companions for roses.

▲ **Rosa** 'Floral Carpet'
◄ **Well-suited companions** for roses include delphinium, peony (Paeonia), beard tongue (Penstemon), and chrysanthemum (Leucanthemum vulgare).

Silver everlasting flower (Helichrysum) *and white dog fennel* (Anthemis) *complement the pastel yellow 'Buff Beauty' rose.*

like a particular combination, don't be afraid to experiment, as long as the plants have similar needs.

The most attractive and satisfying gardens include a combination of complementary and contrasting elements. If you are thinking about companion plantings in your rose garden, consider plants with contrasting foliage or forms and complementary colors. Roses are generally rounded or urn-shaped and shrubby or bushy. Consider mixing them with upright, spiky, even grassy plants, rather than with other shrubs. White, soft yellow, blue, and purple flowers will complement almost every color of rose blossom except for the bright crimson red of some varieties.

Or take the opposite design path. Select plants with complementary foliage and contrasting colors. Go ahead, be brave. Mix bright yellow and blue flowers with your crimson roses. Nature does it in almost every field of wildflowers.

These guidelines also apply to container-grown roses. The roses won't mind, and you can make the containers more attractive if you add low-growing or trailing plants. English ivy (*Hedera helix*) adds interesting and colorful foliage. Moss rose (*Portulaca grandiflora*) and trailing petunias (*P. × hybrida*) provide blankets of charming flowers in complementary or contrasting colors.

Complements and Contrasts

You have an almost endless choice of companion plants from which to choose, whether you're designing a rose garden or a garden with roses. Here are some general guidelines to follow and some plant combinations to consider before you begin designing your garden. If you

*Plants with contrasting shapes, such as the erect honeysuckle (*Lonicera nitida 'Baggesens Gold'*), make effective companions for roses.*

Smart Tip
Pair Spiky Foliage with Soft Colors

The most pleasing rose gardens include compact ornamental grasses and upright spikes of sun-loving flowers, such as foxglove, veronica, salvia, lavender, larkspur, and blazing-star. Add contrasting foliage and complementary color with bearded iris, daylily, yarrow, nasturtium, tickseed, delphinium, coneflower, aster, and blanket flower.

Plants with gray and green foliage crisply set off the lush white roses at Sissinghurst in England.

Gray, Green, and White

Every year, thousands of tourists visit Sissinghurst Castle in Kent, England, and the famous white garden designed by Vita Sackville-West in 1949. Though not the first white garden, it is undoubtedly the best-known. Describing her ideas for the garden, Sackville-West wrote, "All color must be excluded; it must be all green and white, cool, symmetrical, and severe . . . like those enormous eiderdowns that one finds in old-fashioned French hotels."

Inspired by her work and armed with her advice, many visitors to Sissinghurst Castle return home to create white gardens of their own.

White gardens sparkle at twilight. You may use all sorts of white roses, mingled with other types of white-flowering plants and those with pale green foliage, to create your own white garden. Whether it's a broad expanse within the landscape, or only a small island in a sea of green grass, a white garden can be both a tranquil relief from the glaring heat of the midsummer sun and a glowing oasis in the gathering dusk of evening. A judicious selection of plants ensures that the garden is always in flower.

Sackville-West didn't design her garden around roses, although she did include the climbing version of 'Iceberg' as a principal feature. She used underplantings of wormwood (*Artemisia* spp.), dusty miller (*Senecio cineraria*), lavender cotton (*Santolina chamaecyparissus*), and creeping yarrow (*Achillea ageratifolia*). She planted patches of white regal lilies (*Lilium regale*) and foxtail lilies

A classic white garden sparkles with cascading roses, santolina, marguerite (Leucanthemum vulgare), *and campion* (Lychnis).

(*Eremurus* spp.), foxglove (*Digitalis*), baby's breath (*Gypsophila* spp.), climbing hydrangea (*Hydrangea paniculata* 'Grandiflora'), tree peonies, (*Paeonia suffruticosa*), butterfly bush (*Buddleia nivea*), balloon flowers (*Platycodon grandiflorus*), Japanese anemones, and dahlias.

Other white flowers to pair with roses include summer phlox (*P. paniculata* 'Fujiyama'), sweet alyssum, (*Lobularia maritima*), candytuft (*Iberis* spp.), and impatiens. For contrasting foliage, try ornamental grasses, including black fountain grass (*Pennisetum setaceum*) and the steely gray little bluestem (*Schizachyrium scoparium*).

The Clematis Connection

> " *Rose, rose and clematis*
> *Trail and twine,*
> *Clasp and kiss.* "

Alfred, Lord Tennyson, the Poet Laureate of England, wrote these classic lines more than 150 years ago. Yet, despite this long association of two cherished plants, gardeners on this side of the Atlantic Ocean have only recently realized that the comparatively disease-free clematis and its many delightful color combinations make the rose and the clematis almost ideal companions. Because both plants require essentially the same soil, nutrients, and water, both invariably enjoy the relationship. For the best effect, plant your clematis vine a foot away from your rose, but in a site where its roots will be shaded, because the clematis needs cool soil. Then let it climb up and through the rose, where its foliage and flowers will mingle with those of its companion.

Clematis vines are most frequently used as companions to climbing roses, but most varieties of clematis are rather modest climbers and can be used with medium-size to large shrubs just as well. In either case, don't plant any variety that's too rampant a grower, such as sweet autumn clematis (*C. terniflora*). It's robust enough to match the size of almost any rambling rose, and this clematis will smother most roses on which you grow it.

Choose a companion clematis with two things in mind: flower color and flowering time. Obviously, you want flowers with a color that complements and enhances the color of your rose. And, for the maximum impact, both plants need to be in flower at the same time. On the other hand, remember that a later-flowering clematis can provide a splash of color against a background of greenery after a once-blooming rose is finished flowering.

Pruning Requirements

Clematis plants have different pruning needs. Of the three categories of clematis, Group II and Group III clematis are better companions for most roses because of when they are pruned.

A perfect couple: Purple clematis and yellow roses intertwine on the metal arches.

Functional and attractive: 'Floral Carpet' rose cools the roots of Clematis jackmanii, *while providing a splash of contrasting color at its base.*

Group I. These clematis flower on short stalks rising directly from leaf axils on stems produced the previous season (old wood). Because you have to wait to prune until after they finish flowering in the spring, these clematis do not make good companions for any but the once-blooming roses, which generally have the same pruning requirements. Group I clematis include the hybrids of *C. alpine, C. macropetala,* and *C. montana.*

Timing is everything. 'Graham Thomas' blooms with Clematis 'Miss Bateman'.

Group II. This type of clematis flowers in the spring on stems produced from old wood. They often flower again in the fall, just when many *remontant* (repeat-blooming) roses put on their best display of the year.

Prune Group II clematis in the late winter before the buds begin to grow — at about the same time you would be pruning repeat-blooming roses. Clean out weak and dead stems, and cut the others back to a pair of strong, healthy buds. Many of the most popular and dependable clematis are Group II cultivars, including *C. jackmanii*, 'Marie Boisselot', 'Nelly Moser', *C. Henryi,* and 'Mrs. P. B. Truax' among others.

Group III. These clematis produce flowers on new stems each year. Prune these plants in late winter, as you do Group II. Varieties of this group, all of which flower later in the season than Group I or II clematis, include hybrids of *C. Texensis* and *C. viticella;* 'Etoile Violette' is probably the best-known and best-loved Group III. Other dependable Group III varieties are 'Bill McKenzie', 'Comtesse de Bouchaud', and 'Ernest Markham'.

Planting a Clematis and Rose Together

DIFFICULTY LEVEL: EASY

TOOLS AND MATERIALS: Shovel, hose or watering can, bits of cloth to fasten the rose, wire to guide the clematis to the trellis

1 Position the plants in front of the trellis with at least 1 ft. between them; then dig the holes. This spacing ensures ample air circulation between plants.

2 Plant your rose and clematis, and water them well. Tie the rose to the trellis. String the wire across the trellis, and loop the clematis around it.

An Edible Connection

In the Middle Ages, Europeans grew roses primarily as medicinal herbs and food plants. So why not return to those days of yesteryear and plant roses among your culinary herbs and your vegetables? Or, better yet, why not plant herbs and vegetables among your roses?

Of course, you can use roses to spruce up an otherwise mundane vegetable garden. Use miniature roses as a border and larger varieties for a backdrop or boundary hedge. Sometimes the most pleasing effect and the best use of space is to plant vegetables and herbs in the rose garden. To cultivate and fluff the soil, rotate short-term vegetables in the bed. You can grow both annual and perennial ornamental and culinary herbs.

Basil, parsley, salad burnet (*Sanguisorba minor*), sage oregano, anise-hyssop (*Agastache foeniculum*), borage (*Borago officinalis*), coriander (*Coriandrum sativum*), dill fennel, lavender, and thyme are useful herbs that can also serve as decorations in almost any rose garden.

Radishes, beets, turnips, lettuce, tomatoes, cucumbers,

Smart Tip
Combine Roses and Tropical Plants

Mix roses and sun-loving tropical plants, either grown as annuals or dug and brought inside for the winter, to create some unusual combinations and for the satisfaction of challenging your climatic restrictions.

For example, the dark, multi-hued foliage of duck's-foot coleus (*Solenostemon scutellarioides*) complements beautifully the pastel pinks and yellows of many roses. Otherwise, star-cluster (*Pentas lanceolata*), scaveola, golden-trumpet (*Allamanda*), small-flowered tropical hibiscus (*H. rosa-sinensis*), and cape leadwort (*Plumbago auriculata*) are equally pleasing companions for roses.

For vertical interest, add pillars, tripods, or trellises, and drape them with vining plants such as mandevilla and esperanza (*Tacoma stans*).

bush beans, onions, celery, chard, and peppers are among the many vegetable crops that you can grow among your roses.

Some vegetables protect roses from pests and diseases. That's especially true of the alliums. Garlic, garlic chives, kitchen chives, leeks, and all sorts of ornamental alliums provide an attractive contrast in foliage, and their globes of tiny flowers seem to especially complement roses.

In addition to their visual compatibility, alliums and all umbelliferous plants feed beneficial insects, which naturally control the pest population.

Onions (foreground) protect roses from pests; roses dress up the vegetable patch.

Beneficial Companions

Through the ages, many plants have been said to have a beneficial effect on other plants, roses in particular. These are the plants that, according to garden lore, will help protect roses from the onslaught of pests and diseases. Unfortunately, most of this information is purely anecdotal and has never been properly tested by qualified scientists. Still, some combinations are worth trying.

For instance, the herb rue (*Ruta graveolens*) is commonly considered to be an insect repellent, which is especially effective against Japanese beetles. Geraniums (*Pelargonium* spp.) are said to have the same quality. Parsley may help protect roses against other kinds of chewing beetles, and tomatoes are supposed to protect roses from black spot.

Marigolds (*Tagetes* spp), grown for several seasons in the same spot prior to the time you plant your roses, will discourage root-knot nematodes. But marigolds are known to attract spider mites.

All members of the allium family are said to be beneficial to roses, protecting them from aphids, spider mites, black spot, and powdery mildew. Garlic and onions have been planted for many years in the fields of damask roses around Kazanlik, Bulgaria, to increase the scent and to yield more-concentrated essential oils.

Claims for the benefits of growing alliums with roses have been at least partially tested and found to have some merit. For reasons largely unexplained, the edible alliums — garlic, chives, garlic chives, and onions — have demonstrated varying degrees of effectiveness against

Alliums earn their keep in the flower bed. Garlic chives can eliminate spider mites, reduce aphid damage, and protect roses against black spot and powdery mildew.

aphids and spider mites. And, in at least one controlled experiment, when planted underneath roses, garlic chives completely eliminated spider mites and significantly reduced the aphid population. However, effective control of black spot or powdery mildew by planting alliums with roses has yet to be proved.

Herbs and roses have been planted together for centuries. Lavender attracts beneficial insects, which control the pest population.

Dividing and Replanting Chives

DIFFICULTY LEVEL: EASY

TOOLS AND MATERIALS: Shovel, pitchfork, hose or watering can

1 Before or after the plant flowers, dig the chives out of the ground. Plunge a pitchfork into the root mass to divide it in two.

2 Replant one of the chive divisions near the rose. Chives are shallow-rooted and won't interfere with the rose. Water the chives well.

No-No's and Better Nots

Some plants do not make good companions for roses. These plants compete too vigorously for water and nutrients, have incompatible soil or water requirements, or attract too many insect pests.

Don't place plants with strong, woody feeder roots too near your roses. Try to plant your roses some distance away from the feeder roots of preexisting woody shrubs and

This rose is planted too closely to the tree. Woody plants hog water and nutrients and are not good companions.

trees, including many of the shrubs commonly used for formal hedges, such as hollies (*Ilex*), Christmas berry (*Photinia* spp.), yews (*Taxus* spp.), privets (*Ligustrum*), and the like. Some landscapers include boxwoods (*Buxus* spp.) on this list of verboten plants.

Shallow roots and a tidy growing habit make germander (Teucrium) a good choice to grow as a clipped hedge in formal rose gardens.

Look for shallow-rooted companions. You can plant roses and boxwoods together as long as you maintain a stem-to-stem separation between plants of at least 1½ feet. Boxwoods have been used successfully as clipped borders for rose gardens for generations, probably because they have such shallow root systems.

If that's a problem and your climate allows, substitute shrubby germander (*Teucrium*) for boxwood. Germander roots easily from cuttings; it has attractive blue flowers in late spring; and you can shape it to form a low, rounded or even square-cut edging or border.

Rhododendrons and roses do not grow well in the same soil. Although this pair looks fine, one plant will eventually suffer from an improper soil pH.

Plant roses away from a tree's drip line. When you plant a rose near a mature tree, always place it well outside the drip line or up close to the trunk, between the large roots. Don't plant your rose in a shady location.

Acid-Lovers and Roses Don't Mix

Don't try to grow roses with plants that require acidic soil conditions, such as azaleas (*Rhododendron* spp), rhododendrons, and gardenias. Everything may survive, but if the roses are happy, the other plants won't be. And if the others are happy, your roses will never live up to your expectations.

Xeriscape plants don't make good companions for roses. Don't expect xeriscape plants to do well with roses. If you include plants with low-water requirements, such as lamb's ear (*Stachys byzantina*), hens-and-chicks (*Sempervivum* spp.), ice plant (*Mesembryanthemum crystallinum*), black-foot daisy (*Melampodium leucanthum*), and stonecrop (*Sedum* spp.), you'll need to water your roses separately with soaker hoses or with a drip irrigation system. That way, the roses can get the water they need, and the desert plants won't drown. Of course, it goes without saying that the opposite situation also prevails. Don't use bog plants in a rose bed.

Avoid wild portulaca near roses. Moss rose makes an attractive and useful ground cover under roses. However, stay away from the wild form, known as purslane (*Portulaca oleracea*). It makes a nice ground cover and keeps the topsoil loosened just as its cultivated cousin. For that reason, and because it's edible, some rosarians let it grow naturally. But that's almost always a mistake.

Purslane shows up in late spring or early summer and soon breaks out with a flush of small, innocent-looking yellow flowers. Then, only about two weeks later, the tiny little seeds mature, and copious amounts are thrown about the bed. A week later, they germinate. Before you realize what's happening, there's a thick mat of purslane competing with your roses for water and nutrients. It's much more prudent to stick with the more docile, cultivated variety.

Purslane grows into a thick mat, and can suck water and food away from your roses.

The low-water needs of lamb's ear are not compatible with the frequent watering roses require.

Stay away from columbines and marigolds. It's best not to mix either columbines (*Aquilegia* spp.) or marigolds with roses, because each attracts spider mites. However, if you have a problem with root-knot nematode, try marigolds for one season. But be sure to plant chives nearby to counteract the marigolds' tendency to attract spider mites. Annual verbenas (*Verbena* × *hybrida*) also attract spider mites. If you want to add verbenas to a bed of roses, always choose one of the perennial types (*V. peruviana*, *V. tenuisecta*, or *V. erecta*, for example).

CHAPTER FIVE

Rose Culture

*R*oses have the unfortunate reputation of being hard to grow. Many gardeners believe that any rose they plant is going to require special care that is outside their capabilties. But that simply isn't so—the majority of roses don't require extra care, nor do they deserve this poor reputation. If a particular cultivar grows well in its location, it does not require heroic measures to stay healthy and productive. Exceptions occur only when a rose is not suited to local conditions. In the harsh climates in which some of us garden, certain plants cannot survive without special care. But that simply means that gardeners must take the local situation into account when they select their plants—even their roses.

▲ *'Carefree Delight'*

◄ *Roses* in this border are no more difficult to care for than any of the other plants here.

Choose roses *according to their environmental requirements. This 'Illusion' rose thrives with only routine care because it is suited to the climate where it grows.*

Rose Requirements

Roses need good drainage and lots of sunshine, nutrients, and water—needs that you can easily satisfy by siting them in a sunny spot, incorporating sufficient organic matter into the soil, and feeding and watering them properly. If you choose roses that are suited to their environment—and you care for that environment by using mostly organic fertilizers and minimizing or eliminating chemical insecticides, miticides, and fungicides—your plants will require little-more care and attention than any other flowering shrub.

Routine Care

Healthy roses depend on a steady supply of balanced, slow-release nutrients. The most efficient and consistently dependable way to provide this supply is by using organic fertilizers and mulches. All through the season, microorganisms in the soil break down and transform these materials into forms that the plants can use. As an added bonus, this is also the easiest and most economical way to fertilize your plants.

If you want to grow roses primarily for their beauty and for your own enjoyment, you can adopt a somewhat leisurely approach to fertilizing them. Spread a well-balanced, organic fertilizer around the plants at the rate of 20 to 30 pounds per 1,000 square feet of soil area. Apply the fertilizer in the early spring, just as the plants begin growing, and mulch over it.

The 'Suzy Q' miniature roses *in this garden site are low-maintenance because they are well adapted to the climate.*

Using manures and other fertilizers. Aged manures, bagged or not, also make good general-purpose fertilizers. However, if you have a clay soil—and especially an alkaline clay soil—it's best not to use any type of manure more often than once every three or four years because excess soluble salts can build up with more frequent use. (Excess soluble salts interfere with nutrient take-up and water absorption.) If you choose a synthetic fertilizer, look for one with a 3-1-2 or 4-1-2 ratio. When using these fertilizers, you will need a soil analysis every two years.

Mulch for nutrients. Once you have added fertilizer to the soil, mulch the whole area with at least 2 or 3 inches of a coarse-screened compost. Over the next few months, earthworms, fungi, bacteria and other soil organisms will decompose these materials and slowly incorporate them into the soil. When the mulch begins to disappear, that's your signal to do it all over again—apply more fertilizer and another layer of mulch. In regions with long, hot summers, gardeners may make three fertilizer and mulch applications a year. In cooler regions with shorter summers, one application a year usually suffices.

Intensive fertilization. When you grow roses for exhibition and competition, you'll need to make an exception to this easy fertilizing routine. Rose plants require a more immediately available nutrient supply and more frequent feeding to produce the largest possible flowers. You'll want to fertilize them at least once a month, if not more frequently, with a soluble synthetic fertilizer, preferably with an N-P-K ratio of 3-1-2 or 4-1-2.

You'll also want to keep them mulched with 2 or 3 inches of compost, straw, pine needles, shredded leaves, or finely ground hardwood. It's important to get a soil analysis at least once a year when you are using soluble fertilizers. Use the analysis to adjust the fertilizers each year so that you are supplying all of the essential elements without building up an imbalance of any major or minor nutrients. An analysis also tells you whether or not you need to adjust the soil pH or correct deficiencies of minor and trace nutrients such as magnesium, iron, calcium, and sulfur.

Compost *is such an ideal fertilizer for roses that it's worth setting up a bin in an unobtrusive spot in your backyard.*

Earthworms *are excellent indicators of the amount of organic matter in your soil. If worms are numerous, the levels are probably high enough to sustain your roses.*

Organic advantages. When you use organic fertilizers and mulch, nutrients are released primarily by microbial action; there are few excess mineral salts, and leaching losses are small. You can also fertilize any time of the year when the soil is clear of snow. When the soil is too cold for your plants to be active, the soil microbes are also inactive. So the organic materials are not broken down. When the soil warms in the spring and the plants start growing, the microbes begin making nutrients available to the plants. Nature's annual cycle repeats itself with only a little help from you.

Watering

After rose plants have been in the ground for three or four years, they become extremely drought tolerant, especially if they're growing in clay-based or loamy soil and are fed with slow-release, organic fertilizers. A layer of coarse-screened compost or very finely ground hardwood mulch adds to the resilience of a well-developed root system — it keeps the soil cooler and helps to preserve moisture. Mulch also helps prevent the weeds that compete with your roses for moisture.

Despite their drought-tolerance, no water-stressed rose plant is as healthy, vigorous, or freely flowering as it is when it grows in consistently moist soil. In soil with good drainage characteristics, it's almost impossible to water a rose too much or too often.

However, roses cannot tolerate wet feet. The swamp rose (*Rosa palustris*) is almost the only exception to this, but even it won't last long in truly waterlogged soil.

Moisture requirements. Roses thrive when the soil throughout the root zone remains evenly moist, with the pores half-filled with water and half-filled with air. In most soils, this means that the roses will need about 1 to 2 inches of water, including rainfall, every week. In very sandy soils, you may have to add 1 to 2 inches every two or three days to keep the soil adequately moist. However, you can reduce this requirement by mulching heavily and incorporating more organic matter into the soil.

Soaker hoses are ideal for rose gardens because they moisten the soil without wetting the leaves.

Organic mulches retain soil moisture, supply nutrients by feeding microorganisms, and keep weeds in check.

Disease susceptibility. Fungal diseases are always a threat to roses, even in arid regions. Fungal spores are splashed about by water and require high humidity — and sometimes wet leaves — to germinate. So it's always better to water your roses without wetting the foliage. But when that's impossible, try to water very early in the morning so that the foliage will dry off as quickly as possible.

Otherwise, use carefully placed soaker hoses for watering groups of roses. To water any single rosebush or climber, it's efficient to let water dribble slowly from the end of a garden hose onto the soil around the plant.

Drip Irrigation

A drip irrigation system is, with little doubt, the best means for watering a bed of roses. While it was once mandatory to go to specialized suppliers for these systems, you can now buy the necessary components at

Drip irrigation systems may have in-line emitters, as pictured here, instead of small feeder lines.

Smart Tip
Installing Irrigation

If you're installing a complex system, it's best to work with an irrigation company because they will design and guide you through the installation process at no cost. But if you are irrigating only a bed or two, you can do it yourself.

almost any large garden center or store specializing in home-improvement tools and supplies.

Instruction booklets are usually available wherever supplies and components are sold, but fundamentally, a drip irrigation system consists of a main trunk line and smaller diameter, feeder lines, or spaghetti tubes. Water drippers, or emitters, on the ends of the feeder lines carry water to specific garden areas or individual plants.

Drippers are commonly rated (and labeled) according to the gallons of water per hour they deliver. You can vary the amount of water you apply to each plant by using drippers with different ratings and by setting different numbers of drippers around particular plants. As a rule, though, each

Installing a Drip System

DIFFICULTY LEVEL: EASY

TOOLS AND MATERIALS: Drip system components, manufacturer's hole punch

1 *Manufacturers give directions* and supply a specific hole punch for setting up drip systems with spaghetti tubes and emitters.

2 *Similar water requirements* allow both potted plants and roses planted in the ground to be watered with the same system.

rose requires a minimum of three drippers to keep the entire root area properly moistened. In loose, fast-draining soils, rose plants may require four or five drippers each. Drip rings are also available for use in soils where you need even more coverage.

Tie your drip irrigation system to the household water system, or simply attach it to a garden hose. If you choose to attach it to the hose, place a removable filter between the hose and the system. A positive shutoff valve on the connector prevents insects, dirt, and other debris from getting into the lines and plugging up the drippers. Local ordinances may also require a backflow preventer and a pressure regulator, but these are standard components wherever drip irrigation systems are sold.

These systems are not only flexible and easy to design and install but also relatively inexpensive. Even at twice the cost, a drip irrigation system is still a bargain. It pays for itself in the savings given by lower water use and a greatly reduced incidence of fungal diseases.

Watering Roses in Containers

To successfully grow a rose in a container, never let the soil completely dry out. This may mean that you water all but the very largest containers at least every day—or twice a day in very hot weather. But once every day or two may be adequate if the container is filled with a good-quality organic potting soil and if it is watered correctly.

Unfortunately, many people water so quickly that they don't get all of the soil wet — it shrinks, cracks and pulls away from the container. Then, at the next watering, it runs down the sides, leaving much of the remaining soil dry. Harmful soluble salts may also build up as a consequence of poor watering; the only way to get rid of these excess nutrients is to leach the soil by irrigating so much that water runs freely from the drainage holes, taking the salts with it.

Good watering technique. To water a container correctly, let the water run slowly until no more air bubbles appear on the soil surface, and water drips from the drain holes. Then, and only then, can you be certain that you've completely saturated the soil.

Air bubbles should appear any time you water a container. If they don't show up at all, either your soil is waterlogged, or it is still saturated from the last watering, and you are watering too often. If you decide that your soil is waterlogged, check to be certain that the drainage holes aren't plugged. If that isn't the problem, replace the soil with a mix that has better drainage.

A white residue on the soil surface or the outside of the pot is a signal that excess soluble salts are building up in the soil and that it's time to leach it.

Disaster Protection

In Zones 3 and 4 and cold parts of Zone 5, grow own-root roses whenever possible. If the top of the rose is killed, you have a decent chance that it will resprout from the roots. When you must grow a budded rose, place the bud union at least 3 inches below the soil line.

'Rêve d'Or', a tender noisette, won't survive in harsh climates with protracted below-freezing temperatures.

Preparing for Winter

Winter protection is necessary for roses that grow where temperatures drop much below freezing. In regions where temperatures are often well below zero, it takes draconian measures for some types of roses to survive and flower again. Of course, this also points to an obvious solution—choose to grow only those cultivars that are adapted to your climate.

Don't try to grow noisettes or hybrid chinas in Minnesota or Maine. Instead, choose roses that are cold-hardy in these climates—rugosas, albas, and the Buck shrub roses. Many cultivars in these groups flourish with little or no protection in temperatures as low as -30°F.

In any climate, true winter protection begins during the summer. Give your roses adequate sunshine, nourishment, and water. Healthy plants are much better equipped to deal with the onslaught of winter temperatures and winds and can withstand several-degree-lower temperatures than roses that have been weakened by a stressful summer.

The second step in winterizing is to time cultural care well. Stop applying nitrogen fertilizers six weeks to two months before the average date of your first killing frost. Quit trimming and deadheading six weeks before that date. This allows the newest growth to mature so that your roses will harden off properly and go dormant during the first two or three weeks of freezing temperatures. Dormant tissue is less susceptible to tearing when ice crystals form inside the cells.

Mulch plant crowns with a layer of shredded hardwood bark to give extra winter protection in areas where snow cover is erratic.

Wind protection. Winter winds can severely damage roses by virtue of their drying effect, even in regions that aren't subjected to extremely cold temperatures. When the canes are whipped about by the wind, the roots may loosen or even tear.

Tie the longer canes loosely in a bundle with soft rope to alleviate most of this problem. If you live in a region where roses stay dormant all winter, you can even prune a few inches from the longer canes. But wait to do this until after they've been subjected to freezing temperatures for at least a couple of weeks.

Don't do any fall trimming if you live in a region where cold periods are interspersed with warm intervals. Trimming stimulates growth; if the roses break dormancy, the tender buds might begin to develop.

Climbing roses present a special problem. The best approach for winter protection has several steps. Release the canes from their supports, and trim them. Then tie the canes into bundles with soft rope, and wrap them with burlap (never plastic). Secure them so they don't blow around in the wind. You can also dig a really big trench and bury the canes for the winter.

The New Season. Carefully remove the winter protection from your roses just after the average date of your last killing freeze. Do this as early as possible, but remember

Temperatures *that routinely drop to or below the level your roses can safely tolerate call for extra protection. In the fall, mound garden soil loosely up over the plant crown to a depth of 8 to 10 in.*

If snow covers *your garden all winter, you may not need to add any other protection. But if you get a sudden thaw, cover or mulch the roses before all of the snow melts.*

Smart Tip
Extreme Measures

If you grow a rose not adapted to your climate, surround it with a chicken-wire cylinder filled with loosely packed straw or shredded leaves, or fill a commercial rose cone with insulating material.

You may need to bury very tender roses. Dig under the plant just enough to loosen the root system. Then dig a deep trench alongside, and gently turn the rose over into it. Cover it up, pile at least a foot of hay, straw, or compost over the top for insulation, and hope for the best.

that late freezes can destroy the new growth that appears as soon as the plants feel the warmth of spring. Prune as directed on pages 73 to 79, shaping and removing wood that was killed or damaged during the winter.

Lastly, unless your garden is buried under a perpetual snow cover, don't forget that roses must not completely dry out. Even in the midst of winter, be prepared to water if the unfrozen soil begins to get too dry.

Pruning, Trimming, and Deadheading

Every rose plant needs some pruning and trimming. If you neglect these jobs, the plant is not likely to stay healthy or flower well.

Heavy pruning tends to stimulate fewer but larger flowers, the sort you want for exhibition and competition. By the same token, lightly pruned roses usually have thicker, denser foliage and a larger number of slightly smaller flowers on shorter stems. If you prune too lightly, the inside wood of your roses may become crowded, worn-out, and more susceptible to fungal diseases and humidity-loving pests such as caterpillars.

There is no absolutely correct or incorrect way to prune a rose. So the first rule of pruning is this: don't make too big a deal out of it. Follow a few sensible guidelines, and always use the proper equipment.

Prune canes by cutting about ¼ in. above an outward-facing bud. Angle the cut parallel with the bud or at a 45-deg. angle. This allows rainwater to run off the cut surface rather than pooling and creating an incubator for fungal diseases.

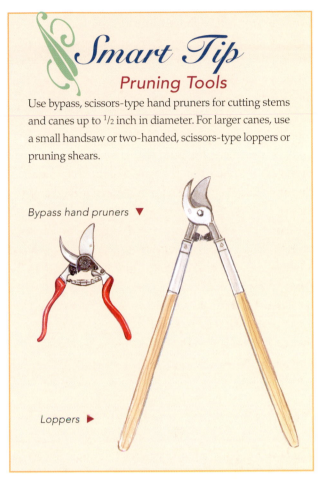

Smart Tip
Pruning Tools

Use bypass, scissors-type hand pruners for cutting stems and canes up to ½ inch in diameter. For larger canes, use a small handsaw or two-handed, scissors-type loppers or pruning shears.

Bypass hand pruners ▼

Loppers ▶

Sensible Guidelines

Prune a rose with a bud union after one full growing season, but wait for two or three years before you severely prune a rose growing on its own roots.

Begin your pruning in spring by entirely removing any dead canes and dead stubs on live canes. Then clean out any weak or spindly growth and any crowded canes.

Make cuts at a 45-degree angle about ¼ inch above a dormant or sprouting bud when you prune or trim a live cane or stem, even when you are *deadheading*, or removing spent flowers.

Whenever possible, cut above a strong, outward-facing bud so that new shoots will grow in a direction away from the center of the plant. But feel free to select a bud that will force the new growth in the direction that suits you (and will result in a shapelier plant).

As a general rule, move down the cane and make

your cut just above a leaf with five leaflets. However, some rose cultivars only have three leaflets per leaf, and others have seven or nine or more. So, when necessary, make your cut just above a healthy leaf at any place that suits you, whatever the number of leaflets.

You can deadhead a rose simply by pinching the old flower off at its base. Formal experiments have shown that it won't mind a bit and will go on putting out new growth and flowers just as if you had followed the rules and cut it above a leaf with five leaflets.

Pruning Time

A gardener's old saw says to prune all bush or shrub roses before the buds begin to break in early spring but to wait to prune climbing roses until after they have bloomed.

This wasn't a bad rule when it came into being. At that time, most of the popular garden roses were repeat-

◀ **Prune all roses** *in spring by removing dead, damaged, diseased, and weak canes and those that cross the center of the bush.*

◀ **Prune repeat-flowering roses,** *including the climbers, while they are dormant. In spring, trim them, and tie the canes to horizontal supports.*

Once-flowering roses *bloom on "old wood"—the canes that grew the previous season. Prune them just after they bloom to give the plants time to grow.*

flowering and bloomed on new wood that grew during the same flowering season. In contrast, most climbing roses of that time bloomed only once, early in the year, on old wood that had grown during the previous season. Because of this, when climbing roses were pruned early, too much of the flowering wood was removed.

Contemporary pruning times. Today, most climbing roses are repeat-flowering and bloom on new wood or on both old and new wood. Prune these plants in late winter or early spring, as you do other repeat-flowering roses. Also, some once-flowering bush and shrub roses bloom on old wood and shouldn't be pruned until after they've finished flowering. Therefore, it's more appropriate to base your pruning schedule on whether your rose blooms repeatedly during the season or only one time, early in the year; that is, whether it blooms on new wood generated this year or old wood that matured the previous year.

In regions where roses don't experience the cold temperatures and winds of winter—but only in those regions—you can trim them as much as necessary any time after they've gone dormant and have hardened off.

Hybrid tea roses *are pruned quite severely in late winter each year.*

But this trimming isn't a substitute for the more formal pruning that you'll do later in the spring.

Repeat-flowering roses. Formally prune all your repeat-flowering varieties—whether they are modern or antique, bush or climbing—in late winter or early spring. Local rose societies often announce when the proper time has arrived, but you can also gauge it as Cynthia Dreibak wrote in 1927,

> *When the forsythia are dressed in golden posies,*
> *Get out those secateurs and prune your roses.*

After that main, first pruning, deadhead repeat-flowering roses, and trim them lightly throughout the flowering season, up until about six weeks before the expected date of the first hard freeze.

Once-flowering roses. Prune all your once-flowering roses—most species roses, ramblers, and old European garden roses, as well as some climbing roses, both old and modern—in late spring or early summer, as soon as possible after they've finished flowering. This gives them a long season to develop wood that will bloom the next year. During the late winter pruning, they can be trained and cleaned up with a light trimming. Because most of these roses will flower on wood that grew the previous summer, retain as much of it as possible.

'Rosa Mundi', *(Rosa gallica versicolor), is pruned after it blooms.*

Pruning by Type and Habit

Though roses are officially divided into two general categories: Modern Roses and Old Garden Roses, pruning methods differ depending upon plants' inclusion in groups that rosarians casually and informally refer to as "antique roses" or "modern roses."

The term "antique rose" has become a very general and all-embracing name for almost any type of rose not typical of the form and habit of the hybrid teas, floribundas, and grandifloras that became so popular during the last half of the twentieth century. They may be once-flowering species roses or old European garden roses, such as albas, centifolias, damasks, gallicas, and moss roses. They may be early repeat-flowering roses, such as chinas, bourbons, noisettes, tea roses, and hybrid perpetuals. Or they may be the even more recently developed, repeat-flowering types known generally as shrub roses, including types such as hybrid rugosas, hybrid musks, David Austin English roses, Buck roses, Meidiland roses, Romantica roses, Explorer roses, Pavement roses, and Simplicity hedge roses.

'Sweet Inspiration', *a floribunda rose, is pruned in late winter.*

Pruning style. As a general rule, it's best to prune the oldest rose types and the cultivars closest to the original species roses the most lightly, and those with a habit and form most like the modern hybrid teas, floribundas, and grandifloras the most severely. But this doesn't have to be a hard-and-fast rule. Experiments by the Royal National Rose Society of England have demonstrated that when most roses are pruned and shaped with hedge shears, just like all the other landscape shrubs, they do just fine.

Pruning hybrid teas and grandifloras. Plants in both of these classes are repeat-flowering and leggy with long flower stems. Prune them in late winter. Remove old, spent canes, and trim the remaining growth by one-third. For larger but fewer flowers, cut out all but four or

Rosa rugosa var. alba, *forms edible hips in fall. Prune in late fall or when the plant is dormant.*

'Peace', *a hybrid tea, is pruned in late winter.*

five of the youngest, strongest canes, and shorten these by at least one-half to two-thirds. Trim any remaining lateral shoots back to one or two growth buds. For display or competition and to improve the size and quality of hybrid tea flowers, remove any side flower buds as soon as they begin to develop during the blooming season.

Pruning floribundas. Floribundas are repeat-flowering roses. They vary in form and habit from leggy bushes to shrub types, but all of them have short-stemmed flower clusters. Prune the leggy varieties in late winter as you do hybrid teas; prune the shrub types less severely, much as you prune modern shrub roses.

Pruning species and wild roses. These roses tend to be once-flowering even though they have a variety of growth habits. Cut out the old, nonproductive wood, and trim the remaining canes by one-third to one-half or more after they flower. Remove untidy canes and deadwood in late winter, and lightly trim long canes at that time.

Pruning gallicas. These roses are spring-flowering and have a low, dense habit. Prune after they flower. Once

'Madame Hardy', *a damask rose, is pruned after flowering.*

the bush reaches a mature size, thin out the old, crowded canes, and trim the lateral shoots by about one-fourth.

Pruning albas, centifolias, damasks, and mosses. These once-flowering plants all have tall, lax growing habits.

'Graham Thomas', *a modern shrub rose, is pruned in late winter each year.*

Shorten the canes and lateral shoots by one-fourth to one-third, and thin out the older, nonproductive wood after the plants flower.

Pruning bourbons, portlands, boursalts, and autumn damasks. These roses usually have some repeat blooms—especially in the fall—on their long, flexible canes. Prune them in late winter by trimming the longer canes by about one-fourth to one-third, shortening the lateral shoots by one-half, and lightly pruning the tips of the remaining canes. Then lightly trim them again after the first blush of flowers has finished.

Prune the four or five varieties of smaller, shrub-type bourbons and portlands in late winter as you do tea roses.

Pruning tea roses. These plants are repeat or almost continuously flowering, and they resemble modern shrub roses. Thin out the old and crowded wood, and shorten the remaining canes by no more than one-third because they tend to resent heavy pruning. Deadhead and lightly trim the plants for shape during the growing season.

Pruning noisettes. Noisettes are repeat-flowering pillar roses and climbers. Remove up to one-third of the older canes in late winter. Shorten the remaining canes by one-third and the lateral shoots to two or three buds. Continue to deadhead and to trim for size and form throughout the growing season.

Pruning hybrid perpetuals. Most hybrid perpetuals are repeat-flowering with willowy, upright canes and some lateral shoots. Prune them as you do modern hybrid teas by removing old, unproductive wood and shortening the canes by up to one-half. Trim the lateral shoots back to two or three buds; then continue to trim severely throughout the season to maximize the flower quantity.

Pruning chinas and hybrid chinas. These perpetual flowering roses have a twiggy, branching habit. Shorten the canes and lateral shoots by about one-third, and thin out crowded and worn out wood on mature plants. Otherwise, just trim and shape these roses as you do any hedge plant.

'Sally Holmes', *a shrub rose, is pruned in late winter.*

'Bonica', *a shrub rose, is pruned in late winter each year.*

Pruning modern shrub roses. These recurrent flowering plants have various forms and habits. When they're two or three years old, begin removing crowded and untidy canes and shortening the remainder by one-third each year. Otherwise, trim for shape and size.

Pruning hybrid rugosas. These plants are repeat-flowering and have a dense, arching habit. The blossoms are followed by colorful hips (fruit). In late winter, thin out the older wood and shorten the remaining canes by up to one-third. The hips mature only if the plants aren't deadheaded. Fortunately, not deadheading doesn't seem to reduce flowering of most rugosa varieties.

Pruning once-flowering ramblers and climbers. Plants in these categories can be quite vigorous and spreading. Remove about one-fourth of the older wood after the plants flower. Prune the remaining canes as severely as necessary for size and form, and trim the remaining lateral shoots back to two or three buds.

Pruning repeat-flowering ramblers and large-flowered climbers. Deadhead these plants to encourage reflowering. In late winter, remove about one-fourth of the older wood, and trim the remaining canes for size

and form. Trim the lateral shoots back to two or three buds. Otherwise, cut the plant back to the size necessary to keep it in bounds.

'Golden Showers', *a large flowered climber, is pruned in late winter each year.*

Controlling Insect Pests & Diseases

*R*oses suffer damage from insect pests as well as from viral, fungal, and bacterial diseases. Because healthy roses are much less susceptible and/or more tolerant of these attacks, the first step in any campaign against pests and diseases is to provide the proper environment. Give your roses a healthy and nutritious soil, lots of sunshine, good air circulation, and plenty of water. Then, when insects and diseases do arrive, minimize or eliminate the use of man-made chemicals so you can protect and encourage beneficial insects. When you must use synthetic chemicals, follow the label directions to the letter, both for your own health and for the health of the environment.

▲ *'The McCartney Rose'*

◄ ***Good health** is the best insurance a rose has against insect pests and diseases.*

◀ *Manual compressed-air sprayers* are always reliable.

Since those first experiments, other institutions have confirmed these results and have extended the tests, and the work has continued at Cornell University. Commercial growers have found that they can add liquid nutrients to the mixture to enhance its qualities and its usefulness. This has resulted in what has been called the modified Cornell University formula, which can be used as a fungicide, miticide, or pesticide.

Spray Formulas and Products

You might be surprised to learn that research has shown that environmentally friendly sprays are at least as effective as chemical fungicides, miticides, or pesticides. Additionally, an overall program using least-toxic sprays requires less work and is usually less expensive than one based on chemical controls. Three sprays—each of which is recommended in the following discussions of common diseases and insect pests—have proved to be especially useful: the modified Cornell University horticultural oil and baking soda formula, Bordeaux mixture, and neem oil.

Modified Cornell University Formula

Dr. R. Kenneth Horst, a researcher at Cornell University, conducted a series of experiments designed to test the effectiveness of various fungicides for use with, primarily, greenhouse plants. Among the plants and products he tested were roses and sodium bicarbonate—ordinary baking soda—mixed with fine horticultural oil added as a spreader-sticker. He found that baking soda was at least as effective as any of the chemical fungicides he tested.

Mix Your Own

Commercial versions of the basic Cornell University formula are now available by mail order and at some nurseries and garden centers. But you can make your own by adding the following ingredients, in the order listed, to 1 gallon of water. Stir thoroughly with each addition.

Basic ingredients:
   2 tablespoons fine horticultural oil
   1 tablespoon mild liquid soap (not a detergent)
   1 heaping tablespoon baking soda

Optional ingredients:
   1 tablespoon or the equivalent of 8-8-8 fish emulsion/liquid seaweed
   5 - 7 droplets of a liquid plant vitamin mixture
   Bacillus thuringiensis var. Kurstaki (Bt), at the recommended concentration

Baking soda is the active fungicide in the Cornell mixture, but researchers have discovered that the spray works just as well if an equal amount of potassium bicarbonate is substituted for the baking soda. Apply the mixture so that it completely covers the surfaces of the leaflets and canes. As a bonus, the fine horticultural oil smothers fungal spores, insects, mites, and their eggs. It can also prevent spores from attaching to the plant.

Nutritional bonuses. The fish emulsion/liquid seaweed serves as a foliar feed for the plant and repels some harmful insects. But be careful with it. Never mix horticultural oil with a fish emulsion/seaweed product that contains sulfur. The resulting mixture is *phytotoxic*, or injurious to plant tissue. A liquid plant vitamin mixture, available at nurseries and garden centers, also gives plants a nutritional boost.

Pest controls. If your plants are hosting enough caterpillars so that you need to spray a Bt product for control, add it to the Cornell mixture. However, this is rarely warranted, because caterpillar incidence is usually light.

Never mix a chemical fungicide or pesticide with the modified Cornell University spray formula. Many combinations can severely damage your plants, but this is particularly true of fungicides containing chlorothalonil. Don't use them on the same plant within ten days of each other, either.

Spraying guidelines. Before you begin to spray, water your roses thoroughly if the soil is not already moist. If pests are present, scare off most of the beneficial insects, such as ladybugs that might be preying on the pests, by spraying the leaves with plain water and an ordinary nozzle on your garden hose.

It's crucial to spray all pest controls and fertilizers very early in the morning or late in the evening, after your roses are in shadow. To avoid damaging the plants, use the Cornell formula only when the temperature will be 85°F or less for a few hours after you spray. Handheld compressed-air misting sprayers do a good job and allow you to spray both sides of all the leaflets.

You can spray a modifed Cornell formula as often as once every two weeks, but you'll probably find spraying only once a month or even less frequently is adequate. If water still beads up on the leaflets (as it does on the surface of a freshly waxed car), a protective coating of horticultural oil is still on the leaf, and you don't need to spray right away.

Bordeaux Mixture

Bordeaux mixture is primarily a fungicide, but it also repels insects such as flea beetles and leafhoppers. You can buy a commercial version or mix your own, as follows.

Using a plastic bucket only, dissolve 3 ounces of copper sulfate (bluestone) in one gallon of water. Then slowly add 5 ounces of hydrated lime, stirring thoroughly with each addition. The resulting mixture is ready to use as a spray or as a drench without further dilution. After using this mixture, wash your equipment well and store it in a glass or plastic container because it's very corrosive to metals. Also, be careful when handling the hydrated lime because it's very caustic.

Neem Oil Products

Neem oil is extracted from the seeds of the neem tree (*Azadirachtin indica*). It has been used for hundreds of years in India to kill many species of insects, fungi, and bacteria. It causes no harm to larger animals, including humans, but contains a compound, azadirachtin, that disrupts the molting processes of many insects.

Modern products. Today, companies manufacture and sell various neem oil products, of which there are two basic types. Full-spectrum neem oils and neem oil extracts contain 0.9% or more

Spots on these rose leaves were caused by spraying in hot conditions in the middle of the day rather than by a disease.

of azadirachtin. Depending on the concentration, they have varying degrees of strength as fungicides, insecticides, and bactericides.

A second line of products contains only a trace of azadirachtin. As a result, many of them have about the same action and effectiveness as other oil sprays, but some retain other chemical compounds that also serve as mild fungicides.

Full-spectrum neem oil products also have some systemic action, meaning that they pervade the whole plant when they are sprayed on the leaves or used as a soil drench in neutral and acidic soils. In alkaline soils, they are less effective as a soil drench and tend not to become incorporated in the plant tissues.

Smart Tip
Be Cautious

Try not to spray full-spectrum neem oil or neem oil extracts when your plants are hosting aphids or other small pests because ladybugs and other beneficial insects are likely to be present. Researchers have reported that this spray is lethal to ladybug larvae, such as the one below, and sterilizes or severely reduces the egg-laying capacity of adult ladybugs for as long as ten days after application.

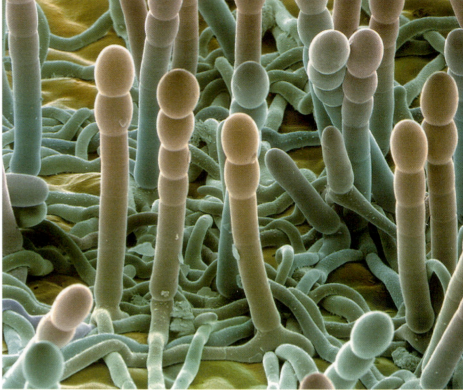

This microscopic view of powdery mildew fungus shows the blue-green mycellium growing on the green leaf and the pale colored fruiting bodies rising above it.

Fungal Diseases

Fungi cause the largest number of rose diseases. Use this as an advantage when you are trying to identify a disease—check this and other references for fungal diseases before looking at those caused by bacteria or viruses.

Powdery Mildew
(Sphaerotheca pannosa *var.* rosae)

This disease is endemic almost everywhere roses are grown because it requires nothing more than cool, humid nights and warm to hot days.

Powdery mildew grows on the top surfaces of leaflets and flower buds. The overly succulent growth that results from excess soil nitrogen is particularly susceptible. Young leaflets develop small blisters and then become covered with a grayish white powder. As they mature, they become

Powdery mildew *always looks like a white powder dusted over the surface of a leaf.*

curled and distorted and sometimes develop a reddish hue. Older, mature leaflets develop a powdery growth but don't usually distort. Affected flower buds open with ill-formed flowers or don't open at all.

Powdery mildew fungi overwinter in both diseased plants and in the soil. Once the weather warms, they spread by wind and splashing water.

Prevention and control. The modified Cornell University horticulture oil and baking soda formula is an excellent preventative and control. Use it immediately after the roses are pruned and then every two or three weeks afterward, or only if you see some infection. Sulfur will kill active infections, but use it only when temperatures will remain below about 85°F for several hours after spraying. Otherwise, it can burn your plants.

Various petrochemical fungicides are also effective. However, you must spray any chemical fungicide at intervals of five to seven days throughout the season. And you should alternate two or more different products, one after the other, so that the fungi don't develop resistance.

Smart Tip
Prevention

Avoid fungal diseases by selecting resistant cultivars, keeping the rose bed clean, pruning and spacing plants for good air circulation, keeping leaves dry when you water, and mulching with compost.

Black Spot (Diplocarpon rosae)

This disease is the bane of rose gardeners, except perhaps in the arid Southwest, where it seldom occurs. It can be a real problem in more humid areas, but humidity alone isn't enough to cause problems. Rain and overhead watering are the usual culprits because leaves must be continuously wet for seven or eight hours before the fungal spores can germinate. Three to 16 days later, brown spots with fuzzy edges appear on the leaflets, enlarge, and develop yellow halos. When an entire leaflet is sufficiently involved, it falls off; a plant can be almost completely defoliated in a relatively short period of time. The optimal temperature for black spot germination is about 75°F. It tends to disappear from the garden when daytime temperatures consistently rise above 90°F.

▲ *Advanced* case of black spot

◄ *Beginning* case of black spot

Common misconceptions. Contrary to common wisdom, black spot spores are not carried by the wind. They are usually transported by splashing water and possibly by insects that move between leaves and plants.

Black spot spores do not overwinter in the soil, in the mulch, or on fallen leaves. They do overwinter in cane lesions.

It's unnecessary to remove infected leaves. As long as they still show green, they're helping to maintain the plant. Similarly, don't cut off a yellowing cane if it carries more than a few leaves.

Prevention and control. Both the modified Cornell University formula and full-spectrum neem oil smother

Smart Tip
Resistance and Tolerance

Some types of roses exhibit considerable resistance to or tolerance for black spot. The rugosa and hybrid rugosa roses, for example, are often said to be immune. But because there are more than 50 different strains of black spot fungi, there are a few locations where even rugosa roses exhibit some symptoms. Other rose cultivars have few or no problems in one locality but act like black spot magnets in others. So if you want to grow resistant roses, ask local rosarians which cultivars to choose.

the spores if you spray when you prune in late winter. If infection does strike, use the Cornell formula every two or three weeks. After using it for a year or two, you probably won't need to spray more than every month or two.

Chemical sprays. Several chemical fungicides are recommended for the prevention or treatment of black spot. Use them at seven- to ten-day intervals, at least until the heat of summer arrives. Sulfur and copper sprays are also effective against black spot and are less disruptive than petrochemical sprays.

Downy Mildew
(Peronospora sparsa)

This fungus is usually found on new growth when the humidity exceeds 85 percent and the temperature is less than 75°F. Purplish red or brown splotches that resemble paintbrush strokes cover the undersides of the leaflets. Eventually, leaves yellow and fall off. You can control downy mildew during cool, humid days by spraying with any of the commonly used oils—canola oil, neem oil, or fine horticultural oil. Bordeaux mixture and lime-sulfur sprays are also effective.

Rust (Phragmidium species)

This serious rose disease most frequently strikes hybrid teas and other roses with large, stiff leaflets. It's a real

problem on the Pacific Coast, although it can show up almost anywhere given the appropriate climatic and cultural conditions. To germinate and enter the leaves, rust spores require a continuously wet surface for at least four hours. Spores remain viable only when temperatures are lower than 85°F.

Rust shows as more-or-less round spots, $1/25$ inch across, that are orange on the underside of the leaflets and a light yellow on the upper surfaces. During the warmest weather of summer, the undersides of the leaflets become covered with reddish orange spots (spores) that are about half the diameter of the earlier ones. After this, affected leaflets wilt and fall off. In cooler climates, rough, black pustules form on both leaf and stem tissues. The disease overwinters in these lesions.

Rust-colored spots make a rust infection easy to identify.

Prevention and control. Good sanitation and timely pruning help to prevent rust. Always remove infected and fallen leaves. Prune before bud break in the spring to reduce the number of spores present. Fertilizers high in potassium may favor this disease. To control it, spray with the modified Cornell formula or dust or spray with sulfur or lime sulfur—three times at ten-day intervals.

Blight (Botrytis cinerea)

This disease is also known as botrytis blight, bud or flower blight, gray mold, and cane canker. It tends to be

▲ **Botrytis blight** makes leaves look as if they are rotting. The spores that grow from rotting spots are gray and fuzzy.

◄ **Flower buds** infected with botrytis may turn tan colored before dropping, unopened.

Dieback (Diplodia species)

Stress, particularly water stress, is the usual cause of dieback. Starting at the tip end and working downward to the base, the affected canes turn brown or black and shrivel somewhat as they die. Since new spore-producing areas are produced in the dead canes, remove all of the deadwood as soon as you recognize the disease. Otherwise, work to improve the overall health and vigor of the plant, and spray with the same formulations used to control black spot.

most prevalent in greenhouses, but it does occur occasionally outside. It causes flower buds to "ball" (fail to open) and to turn a tan color, similar to that of a paper bag. A gray mold may also develop on canes covered with mulch or wet leaves. Prevent this disease with good sanitation and air circulation, and control it by spraying early in the season, three times at ten-day intervals, with copper hydroxide, lime-sulfur, or Bordeaux mixture.

Stem Canker (Coniothyrium fuckelii)

Stem canker can occur on any part of a rose plant—even within black spot lesions on the leaflets—but it's primarily a disease of the canes. It starts off as a small red or yellow spot on the bark that dries out and turns brown as it gets larger. The surface may become wrinkled and then rupture, with dirty masses of tiny, olive brown spores. At the same time, the stem may have died back to that point. All in all, it's not a happy sight.

Insect stings, thorn pricks, or other injuries can trigger this disease. But it usually occurs on a cut cane when you leave a long stub above a leaf bud.

Control stem canker by pruning out infected tissue as soon as you see it. If the disease occurs frequently, stick rigidly to the old rule of making all pruning, trimming, and deadheading cuts just above a healthy bud so that you don't leave long stubs.

Anthracnose (Elsinoë rosarum)

This leaf-spotting fungal disease has been known since at least 1898 and is most common on climbing roses. Small red to purple or brown spots show up first on leaflet tops. Two to four weeks later, reddish brown to light purple spots appear on leaf undersides. The centers of the spots turn an ash-gray with red margins. The leaflets eventually turn yellow or reddish near the spots and develop slits or holes where the spots drop out.

Raised, purple to brown, circular or elliptical spots with sunken middles can also develop on the canes. The fungus overwinters in the cane spots.

Control this disease by cutting out all the infected canes, especially in the spring, and spraying with the same formulas you use to control black spot and powdery mildew.

Spray all surfaces of your plants to eliminate fungal diseases.

Viral Diseases

Roses suffer from a few types of viral diseases, all of which can be serious to life threatening. Insects and infected plants used for propagation are the major vectors of viral diseases. You will learn to recognize their early symptoms as you gain experience.

Rose Mosaic

Several strains of two types of viruses—prunus necrotic ring spot virus and apple mosiac virus—cause rose mosaic. These viruses don't kill roses outright, but they do weaken plants so much that they become vulnerable to temperature extremes that wouldn't ordinarily bother them. Rose mosaic can also cause fewer and poorer quality flowers on shorter stems, a poor transplant survival rate, a reduction in overall size and vigor, and an increase in cane dieback.

Rose mosaic is sometimes called streak because of the pattern it can create on the leaf.

Symptoms. Different cultivars react differently to rose mosaic. Several types of distinctive patterns appear sometimes—but not always—on the leaflets. These include veins that turn red or yellow, white or yellow mosaic or zigzag patterns, or a faint watermarked appearance. The prunus necrotic ring spot virus apparently causes these symptoms, all of which tend to occur early in the year on young leaflets and disappear as the season progresses. In contrast, the apple mosaic strain produces ugly yellow or white blotches on the leaflets that remain visible throughout the year.

Erratic responses. Some rose cultivars exhibit one of these symptomatic leaf patterns every year, while others may show symptoms in some years but not in others. Still other cultivars may never show any outward symptoms at all, which makes it even more difficult to know whether any

*'**Bonica**' is usually disease resistant.*

of your roses are infected.

But you can be almost certain that some of your roses have rose mosaic. Experts think that more than 90 percent of commercially grown roses hosted it in the late 1970s. Due primarily to an industry-wide effort to eradicate the disease, that number dropped to about 50 percent in 1999.

Prevention and control. Other than digging up an infected rose and taking it back to the supplier, a gardener really can't do anything about this disease. Rose mosaic has no treatment, and you can't cure it. When even one leaflet shows symptoms, the entire plant is already infected. But unless the rose is behaving poorly or is dead or dying, this is not always a serious problem. You can just leave it there and enjoy the flowers it offers.

Transmission. This disease is not at all contagious. It won't spread from plant to plant; insects or mites can't carry it; and you won't transmit it with your pruning shears. Rose mosaic spreads only through propagation. Cuttings taken from an infected plant and rooted will result in infected own-root plants. And either infected bud wood or infected rootstocks will result in infected budded plants.

Rose Rosette

Some type of virus probably causes this devastating disease, although no one knows for certain. We do know that it is carried and transmitted by a tiny four-legged eriophyid mite, *Phyllocoptes fructiphilus*. This mite can balloon on the wind and perhaps even catch a ride on a traveling aphid. Once on the plant, it snuggles into the axils at the base of the leaf. The tighter this crevice is, the happier the mite, so shrubby roses tend to make the best hosts. Hybrid teas, with their more open joints, aren't nearly as cozy, so while they are not immune, they are less susceptible. The chief hosts for the eriophyid mite, and thus rose rosette, are wild stands of *Rosa multiflora*.

Hybrid tea 'Taboo' is disease prone.

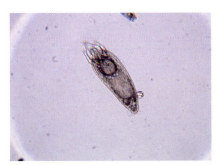

Phyllocoptes fructiphilus, *the tiny carrier of of rose rosette.*

Symptoms. The appearance of rose rosette varies with the cultivar but usually begins with a distorted and discolored leaves — they look as if they have been damaged by a herbicide. Infected canes soon sprout thick clusters (rosettes) of stubby, soft, and brittle stems with elongated leaflets, a growth pattern commonly known as "witches'-broom." On some red-flowered rose plants, the distorted leaflets may be a mixture of lime green and bright red. The stems of diseased plants tend to be thickly covered with soft, comparatively long, rubbery prickles.

A rose may show symptoms of rose rosette in as little as three weeks after inoculation, or there can be an incubation period of a year or more. But once a rose is fully involved, rose rosette is always fatal, killing the rose within 12 to 18 months.

Prevention and control. Symptoms may first appear on only one cane. If you can spot the disease at that point, you can try to stop it — and save the plant — by completely removing that cane. If you don't, the disease will spread quickly. Your only recourse is to remove the entire plant, seal it in a plastic bag, and send it off to the landfill. Otherwise, mites may spread the disease to other rose plants in your garden.

Prevention is the best — and only — cure. This means eliminating the mite and its eggs before any damage is done. But standard miticides aren't effective, because this is a different type of mite — and it's protected down in the tight crevice behind the axillary bud. At this time, the only chemical that has proved effective is dimethoate, a systemic insecticide and miticide. For best results, you must use it as soon as the roses have leafed out in spring and then at no less than 30-day intervals throughout the season.

Horticultural oil, neem oil, insecticidal soaps, and the various seaweed products haven't been effective for treating this mite. However, horticultural oils may help prevent infestations if you spray the bare canes just after the late winter pruning — and after all the old leaves, with their petioles, have been removed.

Transmission. Similar to rose mosaic, rose rosette doesn't appear to be contagious. The tiny eriophyid mite always seems to transmit it. In addition, the fact that a cultivar is budded onto *Rosa multiflora* rootstock has nothing whatsoever to do with its susceptibility to rose rosette — unless, of course, root suckers are allowed to develop into full-fledged plants.

Rose rosette *on young canes.*

Rose rosette *on older growth and buds.*

Insect Pests

Insects love roses almost as much as gardeners do. It's rare to grow an entirely pest-free crop, but if you practice prevention whenever possible and care for your plants well, problems are likely to be slight. Indigenous predators and parasitoids control many pests without your even noticing, and environmentally friendly sprays can control those that escape from their natural enemies.

Aphids

As every grower of roses will attest, aphids can arrive in such numbers that they almost hide the new wood in spring. Also known as greenflies and plant lice, aphids are small, green, black, peachy pink, or brown soft-bodied insects, about 1/8 inch long. They bury their mouthparts in young, succulent growth and suck out the juices. They have yet to kill a healthy rose, although they can weaken

Aphids produce live young when only a few days old.

one severely. They can also transmit some diseases and play havoc with the new growth and the flowers, especially in the spring.

Natural controls. In gardens where chemical pesticides aren't used, the arrival of aphids is a clarion call for ladybugs, green lacewings, syrphid flies, and numerous kinds of tiny beneficial wasps to come racing to the rescue. These beneficial insects immediately begin munching on the aphids but more important, they mate. The larvae of these predators and, in the case of the wasps, parasitoids, eat even more aphids than the adults do. Ladybug and lacewing larvae can eat 40 times their weight in aphids. Spiders, yellow jackets, and resident birds also assist in the cleanup task.

Gardener's controls. Almost any insecticidal spray kills aphids, but such sprays aren't really necessary, and they kill many of the friendly and beneficial insects as well. Instead, try using a hard blast from the water hose. It may be all that's needed. It will wash off most of the aphids, leaving only their mouthparts behind so that they can cause no more trouble.

In the rare cases when you need a spray to eliminate and control aphids, use the modified Cornell University horticultural oil and baking soda formula. This does the trick while also warding off fungal diseases.

Aphids can totally coat the tissues of a plant in early spring.

Spider Mites

These tiny ($^1/_{32}$ inch or less) eight-legged arachnids attack the undersides of leaflets, beginning with those nearest the ground. They breed, lay eggs, and hatch a new generation every five days, so their numbers can multiply rapidly, especially during hot, dry weather. Soon after their arrival, the tops of affected leaflets begin to turn yellow and brown in a salt-and-pepper pattern, finally becoming dry and crisp and falling off the plant.

Two-spotted spider mites are too tiny to see well without a hand lens although you can usually see their damage.

Spider mites create a webbing on the leaves of affected plants, although other types of destructive mites do not.

Spider mites are exceptionally difficult to see with the naked eye, but in large enough numbers they can create a mass of spiderlike webbing on the undersides of the leaflets or between the canes and leaves.

If you don't see webbing but still suspect mites are present, hold a damaged leaf over a sheet of white paper and thump it. If the little specks of dust that fall off begin to move around, you can be sure you have spider mites.

Chemical controls. Conventional insecticides do not control arachnids. You must use pesticides that are labeled as miticides. Even then, exercise some caution; different products have varying degrees of effectiveness, and some rose varieties are damaged if exposed to them.

Environmentally friendly control. Fortunately, chemical controls aren't necessary very often. Because rose plants stressed by lack of water are the ones most likely to suffer from attacks of spider mites, you may be able to prevent problems simply by keeping your rose plants watered.

Spider mites have many natural controls, including ladybugs, lacewings, and several species of mites that prey on the plant-eating mites. Avoid using chemicals to control spider mites so that the beneficials can come to your rescue.

Research has shown that companion planting really does work in the case of roses. Grow garlic chives (*Allium tuberosum*) under and next to rose plants to repel spider mites, once and for all. But don't plant spider mite magnets, such as columbines, marigolds, and annual verbenas, in the vicinity of your roses

If your plants do get attacked, you can often eliminate the pests by simply hitting the undersides of the leaves with a blast of water from the garden hose once every five days. Alternatively, spraying with the modified Cornell University formula or with just horticultural oil can smother both adults and eggs.

Thrips

These small, winged, slender, dark-bodied insects are only about $^1/_{20}$ inch long. Their nymphs are the same size and shape but are wingless and a lighter, yellowish color.

Interestingly, there are more than 600 thrip species, and some of them are beneficial to gardeners. The good guys leave the plants alone and eat moth eggs or prey on mites and other small insects.

Thrips scratch the surfaces and suck the juices from tender young leaflets and flower buds. But the most obvious signs of invasion are distorted flowers with brown or otherwise discolored

Thrips are so small that you'll see their damage first.

edges and flower buds that either fail to open completely or don't open at all. Roses with yellow or white flowers seem to be the most attractive to thrips, but if populations are high, all colors are attacked.

Control. Repeated sprayings with a concentrated neem oil extract or with pyrethrum will control thrips, as will a systemic chemical spray containing acephate. However, by the time the damage is noticed, that generation of thrips has already done most of its damage. So, the best approach is to break the two-week life cycle by destroying the larvae in the soil, along with the adults on the plant. You can accomplish this to a great extent by drenching the soil with beneficial nematodes early in the year and then spraying the young growth and the flower buds with a neem oil extract.

Japanese Beetles

East of the Mississippi River, Japanese beetles are a garden plague, but they can also pose problems in all but a very few of the western states. The adults — blue-green scarab beetles, about $1/2$ inch long, with copper-colored wing covers — seem to arrive in swarms. They chew a garden to pieces for a month or so — always attacking a plant from the top down — and then fly off to return to wherever they came from. But not really. While they're lost to view the remainder of the year, they're living in the soil as fat, grayish white grubs, $1/2$ to 1 inch long. There, they feed on grass (and rose) roots, just like grubs

Japanese beetles can cause serious and unsightly damage.

of the June beetle (or June bug) and the rose chafer, two other common scarab beetles.

Control. When Japanese beetles are busily skeletonizing the leaves and devouring the flowers on your roses, you can spray with full-spectrum neem oil, which will some-times kill or repel them. Otherwise, go out early in the morning or late in the evening—the times of day when they're the most lethargic—and pick or knock them off

Shake the beetles into a cup to save barely damaged blooms.

the plants, and drop them in a bucket of soapy water to kill them.

From a practical standpoint, spraying with neem oil and beetle-picking is about all you can do during the month to six weeks that they're around. Even though pheromone traps are often recommended for Japanese beetles, most people who've tried this approach have decided that the traps don't do much more than attract even larger numbers. So, you'd do better to talk your neighbors into installing traps to lure the beetles into their yards and away from your roses.

A positive and more-definite control can be obtained with milky spore disease (*Bacillus popillae*) and with beneficial nematodes, either one of which can be placed in the soil to attack and kill the Japanese beetle grubs. But unless everyone within about a five-mile radius uses this method, it, too, can only be partially effective.

Rose Midges

These tiny little flies can absolutely devastate a rose garden if they are allowed to go about their business

unchecked. They lay their eggs in young rosebuds and in the tips of tender new growth. The eggs hatch into maggots, which then attack the plant tissue, preventing buds from opening or causing both buds and new growth to become deformed, dry, and crispy, as if they'd been singed with a blowtorch.

Control. Midge pupae live in the soil and can be controlled with beneficial nematodes. You can spray young buds and growing tips with full-spectrum neem oil, which seems to have some repellent qualities and will kill midges and their maggots on contact. Other than those steps, vigilance is the best weapon. Keep a sharp eye out in the spring and fall, when midges are the most active, and immediately remove and destroy any infected flower buds or growing tips.

Rose midges can interfere with normal growth.

Rose Leafhoppers

These pale yellow, winged insects are up to $3/16$ inch long. The nymphs are creamy white and wingless. Leafhoppers suck the chlorophyll out of the leaflets, causing them to develop a pale, mottled look. Eventually, the leaf edges and tips begin to brown and curl, giving an appearance similar to that of salt burn or sun scald. The undersides of the leaflets are often covered with dark excrement and with the white skins cast off by the leafhopper nymphs, confirming evidence of their presence. In addition to this damage, the nymphs may transmit viral diseases.

Rose leafhoppers lay one or two batches of eggs each year in the younger, softer wood of the roses. The punctures made during this activity can cause a pimpled

surface to develop and, if enough twigs are affected, can cause severe damage to the rose plant. Otherwise, outside of the Pacific Northwest, leafhoppers aren't generally considered to be a serious problem. You can

Rose leafhoppers leave pale spots where they have fed.

control them with insecticides and with horticultural oil or neem oil sprays.

Scale Insects

These mealybug cousins attach themselves permanently on a rose cane or stem, forever hidden under small gray or brown oval shells. They insert a pair of strawlike structures into the tissue and suck out the plant juices. If left alone, they can multiply into numbers that are capable of

Scales can form huge colonies.

severely weakening and damaging a plant. But these insects are easily controlled. Just pick or rub them off, or spray the surface with fine horticultural oil.

Caterpillars

Many kinds of caterpillars chew on rose leaflets and flowers, but many of them are the larvae of otherwise desirable butterflies. So you must decide whether or not the damage they do is something you're willing to tolerate. If not, then spraying with a solution of *Bacillus thuringiensis* var. *kurstaki* (commonly known as Bt) will soon rid the garden of caterpillars without harming any of the birds, animals, or beneficial insects. And Bt has another advantage. You can spray only the foliage you want to protect, leaving other plants untreated for the butterfly larvae to munch on.

Incidentally, when you apply a Bt product, you're not actually distributing living bacteria. Bt is a crystalline toxin produced by bacteria and sold either as a liquid spray or as a dust. When ingested by a caterpillar, this toxin affects the digestive tract, and the little beastie quits feeding and dies in a few days.

Caterpillars *don't usually eat your rose buds. Remove them by hand to avoid spraying.*

Control. Birds are an excellent control for caterpillars, as are trichogramma wasps. If you don't seem to have an indigenous population, you buy the wasp eggs at a garden center and place them in your garden. After they hatch and mature, these tiny little wasps will lay their own eggs in butterfly and moth eggs, which will then be eaten and destroyed by the trichogramma larvae. Because several egg-laying schedules have to mesh for all of this to work properly, it's better to distribute modest amounts of trichogramma eggs several times during the season, rather than make one large application.

Cane Borers

These troublesome pests are the larvae of sawflies and carpenter bees. Both insects drill down into the center of

Cane borers *can quickly kill a cane, so watch for damage.*

a freshly pruned cane to lay their eggs, thereby leaving an obvious hole. To get rid of the problem and prevent further damage, either cut the cane off below the base of the tunnel, or chase a small wire down to the bottom to kill the developing larva. Then plug the hole with white glue. You can also use white glue over all your pruning cuts directly after you make them to prevent cane borers from attacking your plants.

Grasshoppers

These garden scourges are most common in hot, arid regions, and their populations are likely to be highest after a relatively mild winter. At their worst, they can descend on a garden and devour every leaf in sight in a matter of days, if not hours. And that includes not only roses and other ornamental plants, but trees, shrubs, and vegetables as well.

Grasshoppers *are serious pests in hot, arid climates.*

Control. Applied broadly, the protozoan *Nosema locustae*, which is sold under several brand names, can be used to significantly reduce the numbers of grasshoppers. But it's useful only to control the young nymphs and has little or no effect on the adults that are doing all the damage. For those, a spray of concentrated, full-spectrum neem oil will kill adults and is said to have significant repellent qualities. Citrus-based products will also kill adult grasshoppers if sprayed directly on them.

In the final analysis, though, the best control for grasshoppers is a healthy bird population. It's for a good reason that there's a monument to seagulls in Salt Lake City.

Cutter Bees

These bees snip perfectly round or semicircular holes in rose leaflets to gather linings for their homes. The damage may look severe, but it's entirely cosmetic and not at all harmful to the rose. Therefore, because all bees are beneficial, and cutter bees are not aggressive, the best approach is simply to admire their considerable skill and let them go about their business.

Cutter bees damage *is unmistakable but not serious.*

Spittle Bugs

These small, light green insects hide themselves in globs of frothy white foam, generally on new growth early in the season. They cause little or no damage to the rose, but their shelters — sometimes called cuckoo spit — are unsightly. So, if they bother you, wipe them off with a handy rag, or wash them off with a blast of water from the hose.

Spittle bugs *are rarely serious pests, but they make plants look unattractive.*

CHAPTER SEVEN

Propagating Your Roses

*P*ropagation is the key to increasing your rose gardens. By using only a few simple techniques, you can easily grow new plants from old favorites. If you move and can't take a treasured rose, you can use your propagation skills to take cuttings from the plant. When a friend has a rose you admire, you don't have to go out and purchase one for yourself. Instead, you can reproduce it by air or stem layering. In cases where you want to grow a particular cultivar on its own roots but can find it only as a budded plant, you can always propagate it to create own-root plants.

▲ *'Cardinal de Richelieu'*

◄ ***Propagating*** *your favorite roses is the least expensive way to add to your collection.*

Propagation Techniques

Stem cuttings, soil layering, and air layering are the easiest and most reliable propagation methods for roses in the home garden. Growing roses from seeds is the least reliable method. For one thing, the only seeds that produce plants identical to their parents are from species roses that have not been cross-pollinated. Additionally, most rose seeds require complicated stratification routines (periods of alternate freezing and thawing).

Propagation of most roses is much easier than you probably imagine. Once you've perfected these techniques, you'll find that the major impediment is legal rather than horticultural. You cannot legally propagate a patented plant for 17 to 20 years past the time the grower introduced it. But you're free to propagate any of the older roses and cultivars that are no longer under patent protection. So it pays to learn the history of a particular cultivar before layering it or taking cuttings.

Cuttings

Cuttings are the most popular way to propagate roses with both home gardeners and professionals who grow own-root roses. The technique is simple, and many cultivars, particularly Old Garden types and species roses, root readily from their stems.

Propagation by Cuttings

DIFFICULTY LEVEL: MODERATE

TOOLS AND MATERIALS: Pruning shears, garden gloves, pruning knife, 3- to 3½-in. peat pots, potting medium, pencil, rooting hormone,

1 *Take a Cutting. Make the cutting from a strong cane that's just bloomed. Cut so that it has four to five leaves. Trim the top at a 45-deg. angle just above the topmost axil. Leave three or four leaf buds farther down the shoot. Cut the bottom at an angle through a junction with a side branch, leaving a "heel" at the base. Immediately place the cutting in water.*

2 *Prepare the Container. Fill a round, 3- to 3½-in. peat pot with a sterile potting medium. Soak the pot in warm water, and allow it to drain. Peat pots allow you to see the roots as they push through the pot. That's a sure sign it's time to repot. You can transplant a rooted cutting, peat pot and all, to a larger container without disturbing the young root system.*

Keep humidity levels high around your cutting by covering it with a glass jar or cutoff plastic bottle until roots form.

Late spring or early summer is the best time to take cuttings because the wood will be at the right stage of maturity to root well. But cuttings taken anytime in the period between the fading of the first flowers and the first fall frost will usually root.

If your cutting doesn't grow roots, don't be too hasty to blame yourself. Despite the simplicity of this technique, it will not work for all roses. Additionally, some of the more recently introduced hybrid tea roses do not have much vigor. Even if their cuttings develop roots, they may grow up to be weak and frail plants. That's the reason some cultivars will always be sold only as budded or grafted plants and never as own-root plants.

Smart Tip
Cutting Length

Rose class determines the optimal length of the cutting. For hybrid teas and bourbons, cut the shoot 7 or 8 inches long; for chinas, floribundas, and modern shrub roses, cut it 4 or 5 inches long; and cut shoots of miniature roses 3 inches long.

Always take three or more cuttings of a plant in case some do not root.

clear plastic 16-ounce cups, permanent marker, aluminum wire, plastic bag, twist-ties, 8-inch or larger pots, and fertilizer

3 Prepare the Cutting. *Press your thumb against each thorn to remove it. (If thorns don't pop off easily, the cane wood probably isn't ripe enough.) Remove all but the topmost one or two leaves; be careful not to damage any of the buds. Snip off all but four or five leaflets. Scrape off the bark at the bottom of the cutting making a narrow 1-in.-long wound, one on each side.*

4 Insert the Cutting. *Punch a hole in the center of the potting medium. Dip the bottom of the wet cutting in rooting hormone powder, and tap off the excess. Insert the cutting into the hole, and firm the soil. Punch holes through the bottom of a plastic cup. Label it with the rose's name, the date, and the source. Slide the peat pot inside the cup.*

Steps continue on page 100.

Propagation by Cuttings, continued

5 **Make a Greenhouse for the Cutting.** *Rose cuttings need constant moisture and humidity. Construct a simple wire framework by looping two or three lengths of wire over each cutting. Insert the ends between the peat pot and the plastic cup. Carefully slide the cup into a clear plastic bag, and seal the top with a twist-tie. Make sure the plastic does not touch any of the leaflets.*

6 **Care for the Cutting.** *Place the cutting in a warm place with bright light but not in direct sunlight. Each cutting will develop differently. You may notice a flush of new growth as the first sign that roots are forming. Or you may see roots push through the sides or bottom of the peat pot. It may take as little as two weeks or as much as six months for roots to develop.*

7 **Transfer the Cutting.** *Transfer the rooted cutting to an 8-in. pot. Add organic potting soil, completely burying the peat pot. Sprinkle a teaspoon of a slow-release, balanced fertilizer with trace elements over the soil. Place the container in cool shade, and keep it well watered. Over the next ten days to two weeks, gradually move it outside until it gets direct sunlight for at least six hours a day.*

8 **Transplant the Cutting.** *Transplant vigorous cuttings into the garden during the first fall in milder climates, and mound soil 4 to 6 in. high around the canes. After the ground freezes, surround the plant with wire mesh, and cover with mulch. In colder climates or for cuttings that aren't mature, keep the plants in containers, and protect them from freezing temperatures until the following spring.*

Soil Layering

Sometimes you'll get better results propagating roses by soil layering than with cuttings. This method, where you bury a cane section so that it develops roots, works only for roses with long and limber canes. Start this project early in the year.

Propagation by Soil Layering

DIFFICULTY LEVEL: **MODERATE**

TOOLS AND MATERIALS: Pruning knife, toothpick, rooting hormone, artist's brush, shovel, staple, potting soil, trowel, mulch, pruning shears

1 Prepare the Cane. *Select a young cane that you can bend to the ground with 10 to 12 in. to spare. Strip off all leaves on the cane except for two or three at the end. Make a 1-in. cut at a point where the cane will touch the ground, just below a leaf bud; angle the cut about a third of the way into the cane. Prop the cut open with a toothpick or a used wooden matchstick. Sprinkle water onto the cut, and dust with rooting hormone powder.*

2 Bury the Cane. *Dig a trench about 4 in. deep, and place the cut portion of the cane at the bottom. Bend the end of the cane upward after it touches the ground. Pin the cane in the trench with a U-shaped staple fashioned from a wire coat hanger. Fill the trench with organic potting soil, burying the cut part of the cane, and tamp the soil firmly. Place a rock over the mound, and add a thick layer of mulch.*

3 Check for Roots. *Keep the area well-watered. Roots should form within six to eight weeks. To check progress, carefully dig down, remove the staple, and gently tug the cane. Resistance means that roots are developing. Cover the area again if the plant is not ready. Once roots are formed and you see new growth aboveground, you can gamble and dig up your new plant, or you can wait until fall or the following spring, which gives it more time to mature.*

4 Dig Up the New Plant. *Use sharp pruning shears to cut the cane off at ground level on the side closest to the original plant but near the new root ball. Wait two more weeks; then carefully dig up the new plant. You can either move the plant to its permanent location if it's vigorous, or transplant it into a container for additional growing time. In that case, provide proper care until the plant is ready to be transplanted to the garden.*

Air Layering

Air layering is another way to propagate otherwise hard-to-root roses. It's a good alternative for roses that have canes that are too short or too stiff for soil layering.

Propagation by Air Layering

DIFFICULTY LEVEL: **DIFFICULT**

TOOLS AND MATERIALS: Garden gloves, pruning shears, pruning knife, toothpick, rooting hormone, sphagnum moss, plastic wrap, twist-

1 **Remove Flowers, Leaves, and Thorns.** *Select a straight young cane that has just flowered. Prune off spent flowers and all but the topmost three leaves. Remove the thorns from a 6-in. section located 8 to 12 in. from the top of the cane.*

2 **Cut the Cane.** *Make a 1-in. cut along the 6-in. section, using a sharp, sterilized knife. Angle the cut about a third of the way into the cane. This wound encourages roots to grow around the opening.*

3 **Keep the Cut Open.** *Prop the cut open with a toothpick or a used wooden matchstick. Sprinkle water into the cut; then dust it with rooting hormone powder. The powder and moisture in the wound encourage root growth.*

4 **Pack in Sphagnum Moss**. *Thoroughly wet a large wad of sphagnum moss, and squeeze out the excess water. Pack the moss thickly around the cut, covering the wound and about 2 in. of wood on each side.*

ties, brown paper, container, and potting soil

5 **Wrap in Plastic.** *Cover the moss-covered cane with plastic kitchen wrap. Use twist-ties or tape to close the openings in the wrap at either end of the wound. Seal it well so that the moss remains damp for several weeks.*

6 **Cover with Brown Paper.** *Tie or tape a loose covering of brown paper over the plastic-covered moss. This will shade it and prevent the sun from turning that sealed plastic bubble into a miniature oven.*

7 **Check for Roots.** *Roots should develop within six or eight weeks, sometimes sooner. To check the progress, temporarily remove the paper covering, and look for any roots visible under the plastic. Also check for signs that the peat moss is drying out.*

8 **Transplant.** *Sever the cane from the original plant. Gently remove the paper, plastic wrap, and ties or tape. Transplant the cane, peat moss and all, to a container filled with potting soil. Transplant to the garden when mature.*

CHAPTER EIGHT

A Gallery of Easy-Care Roses

If you want to grow roses without a lot of extra effort. . . .

. . . and expense, choose those types and varieties that have a proven track record in local gardens.

Start by selecting roses that have been sold at your local nurseries and garden centers for 20 years or more. You can be almost certain that, if a rose is still popular after all that time, it's not only adaptable to your local climate and soil but also has a reasonable tolerance of or even a resistance to the pests and diseases that plague local rose gardens.

Ask local gardeners about new roses. When your fancy is captured by the seductive charms of a newer rose, ask your local rose gardeners about it before you break this 20-year rule. Nothing is more discouraging than to invest two or three years in a rose, only to discover that it just isn't suited to your garden.

After you've gained some experience, you can begin experimenting with new introductions and the many cultivars that entice you from the pages of catalogs, books, and magazines.

Use the gallery as a starting point. This chapter will help you get started with your quest for easy-care, dependable roses. It includes photographs, descriptions,

◀ *Easy-care roses* are suited to many locations.
▶ *R. 'Claire Martin'*

and cultural information for representative varieties of the major types and classes of garden roses. Not every rose mentioned here qualifies under the 20-year rule, nor would all of them be good choices for your garden. But they all have proven track records. Check the zones and the general climate hardiness requirements of any rose that interests you. (The zones noted here are USDA zones. See the hardiness map on page 148.) Some roses are more cold-tolerant than others. And some roses thrive in hot summers, while others do not.

Any rose cultivar can be trouble-free in one region and have serious problems in another. That's why it pays to consult local suppliers and other rose growers.

Mature size depends on length of growing season. Estimates of the average mature sizes are given for every rose described in the gallery. If you live where minimum winter temperatures go below –10° F and have a relatively short growing season, you can expect your mature plant to be smaller—sometimes only half as tall and wide as listed.

If you live where minimum winter temperatures stay above 10° F and have a longer-than-average growing season, then it is likely that your roses will grow larger than described on the following pages—sometimes twice as large.

Gallicas

R. canina is believed to be the parent from which gallica roses evolved.

Description. Most gallica roses are twiggy, suckering shrubs that are relatively late to leaf out in the spring and flower only once in late spring or early summer.

In general, gallicas are extremely cold hardy and can withstand winter temperatures as low as –25°F (Zone 4b) with little or no protection. However, some of the longer-caned varieties will sustain a certain amount of superficial damage whenever temperatures approach that minimum.

Most gallicas grow to be 4 or 5 feet tall, almost that wide, and have very attractive, blue-green foliage, prickly canes and stems. The very fragrant flowers bloom in pink to mauve shades. And because much of their fragrance is retained in the flower petals, gallica roses are ideal for potpourri mixtures.

All in all, gallicas make attractive accent plants, and if their once-a-year flowering is really a problem, they can be used in mass plantings, where you can mingle them with roses that flower throughout the season.

History. Some experts believe that the gallica rose sprang naturally from *Rosa canina*, the wild "dog rose," which is found not only in the Europe of today but also in the fossil record of 35 million years ago. In any case, gallicas are probably the oldest of the European garden roses.

The original gallica rose — the French "Rose of Provins" — probably grew wild both in central and southern Europe and in western Asia in ancient times. There's little doubt that it was the rose of the Medean fire worshipers in Persia in the twelfth century B.C. And it was certainly cultivated in Paestum, the ancient Greek colony and Roman city located near the Bay of Salerno in present-day Italy. Nevertheless, French historians claim that, around A.D. 1260, the original *Rosa gallica* var. *officinalis* was brought to Provins by Thibault le Chansonnier (Thibault the Singer) when he returned from a crusade to the land of the Saracens, known today as Syria.

Gallica roses occupied much of the garden created by Marie-Josèphe Rose Tascher de la Pagerie, more commonly known as Napoleon's wife, Josephine (and as the widow of the guillotined Vicomte Alexandre de Beauharnais), at their chateau called La Malmaison, located just outside of Paris in the village of Reuil. And gallicas were the objects of much hybridization by both French and Dutch growers for many years. It's now estimated that at least 2,000 hybrid varieties once existed, of which perhaps 100 are still around today.

R. gallica *var*. officinalis

'Charles de Mills' is believed to have originated in Germany, although its original developer and date of

'Charles de Mills'

origin aren't known. With upright, arching growth, and a height of 5 feet and width of 3 feet, it has large, fragrant, crimson-to-purple, very double, flat-faced and quartered flowers.

'Belle de Crécy is a lax-growing, almost thornless shrub that grows about 4 feet tall. It has very fragrant, double flowers that open a rich cerise and then fade to

'Belle de Crécy'

mauve and violet tones. 'Belle de Crécy' was reportedly raised by Monsieur Roeser at Madame Pompadour's chateau and introduced sometime before 1829.

Damasks and Autumn Damasks

Description. Fundamentally, there are two types of damask roses, and both types are celebrated for their intoxicating fragrance and for their traditional use as sources of rose attar, an essential oil used in perfume.

Just snuggle your nose among the petals of any damask flower, and you'll discover why these roses have enthralled and mesmerized civilizations throughout much of recorded history.

The once-flowering damasks—sometimes known as "summer damasks"—bloom only in spring or early summer. Even today, these roses are most frequently used for extracting rose attar.

The repeat-flowering damasks, commonly referred to as "autumn damasks," bloom again in late summer or fall, but not with any real profusion of flowers.

Differences. Summer damasks grow taller. Other than their flowering habits, the main difference between the two types is that the summer damasks tend to have more upright canes and, therefore, grow taller. The twice-flowering autumn damasks tend to be more twiggy and shrubby by nature.

Hardiness. All damasks survive to at least Zone 7a, some colder with protection. Both types are cold tolerant without protection to a minimum temperature of at least 0°F (Zone 7a), but they can be grown where temperatures approach −40°F (Zone 3a) if they're mounded over with soil and compost and protected by a significant snow cover.

Damasks are also somewhat more tolerant of high summer temperatures than are the other old European

R. damascena *var.* bifera, *an old repeat-flowering damask*

garden roses, but they also appreciate a winter cold enough to provide them with a period of solid dormancy.

History. There's some evidence that the original once-flowering damask, *Rosa* x *damascena*, resulted from a cross between *R. gallica* and *Rosa phoenicia*, a species rose of the eastern Mediterranean. Without doubt, several varieties of the summer damasks were being cultivated in that part of the world as early as the fifth century B.C.

As with gallicas, French historians claim to have discovered the damask roses. They say the first examples were brought back to Champagne by Robert de Brie when he returned from a crusade to the Holy Land in A.D. 1254

A different union must have resulted in the original repeat-flowering damask, known as *R.* x *damascena* var. *bifera*, which means "twice-fruiting," and *R. damascena* var. *semperflorens*, which translates as "always in flower." Most experts believe that the parents of this famous rose were *R. gallica* and *Rosa moschata*, the late-blooming musk rose of southern Europe and northern Africa, but others believe that it

has much more complicated ancestral lines.

Up until the middle 1700s, the autumn damasks were the only European garden roses that rebloomed dependably. So, everything being relative, it's easy enough to understand how they could be said to be "always in flower." And that can also explain why autumn damasks were known as the "Four Seasons Rose" and the "Twice-Blooming Rose of Paestum."

'Madame Hardy' is a white-flowering damask that some believe must have resulted from a cross with an alba. It was raised in 1832 by Monsieur Hardy in the Luxembourg Gardens and has large, cupped flowers

'Madame Hardy'

with green eyes on upright shoots that grow as long as 6 feet. The plant grows 4 feet wide.

'Rose de Rescht' is listed by the American Rose Society as an autumn damask, although not many experts agree with that classification, at least for the rose that's grown by that name in the United States.

'Rose de Rescht' has few of the traits of a true autumn damask. It seldom grows to be more than 3 or 4 feet tall and is an upright, true shrub, with lovely,

'Rose de Rescht'

Albas and Centifolias

Description. Albas and centifolias are at their best when grown in cooler parts of the country because they seem to resent hot summers and need a reasonably cold winter for proper dormancy. Nevertheless, a few varieties will do moderately well in Zones 8 and 9 if given plenty of water and some protection from the strongest midafternoon sun. Both the albas and the centifolias are sun-loving, once-flowering, and cold hardy, tolerating winter temperatures as low as −25°F (Zone 4b) without significant damage. Both types prefer the cooler parts of the country, with the albas, in particular, resentful of hot summers.

Albas are generally long caned, tall, arching shrubs; whereas, the centifolias are shorter and more varied in style and structure. Neither does well in a shady location.

History. At some time in the future, there will have been enough DNA testing done to know for certain how the albas and centifolias came into being (along with, perhaps, the source of the mutations that produced the moss roses). But for now these are all something of a mystery. Most experts consider that the albas originated from a cross between a summer damask and a white-flowering form of *R. canina*, the old European "dog rose" but no one knows for certain.

(Incidentally, in this context, "dog" is not used in a derogatory way. Some sources say it means "common," as in "easily found." Others claim its thorns resemble a dog's fangs. But the Roman Pliny, in his *Natural History*, says it was given this name because its hips were supposed to "cure the bite of a mad dog.")

It's believed that the centifolias, also known as Provence, or cabbage, roses resulted from crossbreeding gallica, damask, and alba roses, with the wild musk rose. The Dutch are credited with perfecting them with an extensive program of selection and hybridization, beginning about 1580, but they probably originated in Italy at an earlier date.

fragrant, fully double, deep-pink-to-fuchsia-colored flowers snuggled well into the top set of leaflets, more like the typical portland rose. It blooms singly, not in clusters, and it flowers at regular intervals, from spring or early summer and into fall.

Unfortunately, we'll never know the true lineage of 'Rose de Rescht' unless future DNA testing provides that information for us some day. Miss Nancy Lindsay claimed that she brought it back to Europe in 1940 from the ancient caravan stop of Rescht in Iran. She also introduced 'Gloire de Guilan', but cynics say she more likely found 'Rose de Rescht' in a garden in France or Italy.

'Rose de Meaux', named for a town just northeast of Paris, is a much more versatile centifolia, and can be grown with fair success almost anywhere in the United States. It's a small, once-blooming, 3-foot-tall and 2-foot-wide shrub with double pink flowers the size of a silver dollar. It was developed in 1789 and has

'Rose de Meaux'

a 1799 sport, 'Rose de Meaux Blanc', which has white flowers with centers brushed with pink.

'Great Maiden's Blush' seems to be more tolerant of summer's heat and is seen more often than the other albas in the southern part of the United States. But its more suggestive or sensual name, 'Cuisse de Nymphe' ("nymph's thigh"), may have something to do with this. It was painted by Pierre-Joseph Redouté as *Rosa alba regalis* and, when left to its own ends, does indeed make a regal arching shrub, fully 8 or 9 feet tall and 4 or 5 feet wide. Its light pink flowers are double and sweetly scented. It was first grown sometime before 1738 and may date back as far as the fifteenth century.

'Great Maiden's Blush'

Moss Roses

The moss roses are considered by some to be a fifth type of old European garden rose. Named because of the curious, often fragrant, moss-like growth that develops on the buds and flower stems, the roses are essentially two types: those that sported from the centifolias and those that are mutants of damasks, mostly the autumn damasks. From this, some have suggested that mossing originated with the wild musk rose, which is probably an ancestor of both autumn damasks and centifolias.

Moss roses have the same general forms and sizes as the types from which they were bred. Their cultural requirements and their cold and heat tolerances are also essentially identical to the damasks and centifolias.

'Crested Moss' is a once-flowering, centifolia-type moss. Also known as 'Cristata' and *Rosa centifolia muscosa cristata,* it was introduced in 1826 by J. P. Vibert of Angers, France. But according to several sources, it was actually found about 1820 growing on a wall of an old convent in Fribourg, Switzerland.

In France, this rose is known as 'Chapeau de

Napoléon,' a name that best describes its main charm. The mossy growths are only on the edges of the sepals

'Crested Moss Rose'

of its flower buds, where they create a shape that resembles Napoleon's distinctive hat. The mossed buds open to become cupped and wonderfully fragrant, clear pink double flowers on a loose, well-foliated, 5-foot shrub.

China Roses

Description. These repeat-flowering roses were the breeding stock for all the Old Garden Roses known today as china roses. Unfortunately, however, they and their progeny are difficult to grow in regions colder than Zone 7. But they don't mind heat at all and are popular and dependable roses for southern and southwestern United States gardens.

History. When Robert Burns wrote, "Oh, my love's like a red, red rose that's newly sprung in June," he was still unaware of any other kind. His roses bloomed only in late spring or early summer, unless he was fortunate enough to have an autumn damask or a late-blooming musk rose in his garden. And he was, of course, referring to pink roses.

Europeans cherished their garden roses for centuries, even though, with those few exceptions, none of them flowered for more than a few weeks each year. So it's easy to understand the excitement generated when the first truly repeat-flowering roses arrived on sailing ships from the Orient.

It's now generally accepted that the first to arrive was the Chinese garden rose known today as 'Old Blush'. At that time, however, it was known by many names, including 'Parsons Pink China' 'Old Pink Monthly', 'Old Pink Daily', and *Rosa chinensis*.

It's believed that this Chinese rose arrived in Sweden in 1752 and in England soon after that. Still, records of that time are often incomplete or missing entirely, and 'Old Blush' or a very similar rose appears to have been included in an Italian painting as early as 1529. Some researchers also believe there is evidence that this rose was being grown in the gardens of one or more of the great manor houses of England by the sixteenth century. It's certainly old enough because it appears in Chinese paintings hundreds of years old.

It's generally agreed that the next repeat-flowering Chinese rose to arrive in Europe was some version of 'Slater's Crimson China', also known as 'Old Crimson China', "Chinese Monthly Rose," *Rosa bengalensis*, *Rosa chinensis semperflorens*, and *Rosa indica semperflorens*. Most sources say that this rose was brought to England about 1790 or 1792, but even that's not certain, because the herbarium at the British Museum apparently has a dried specimen that's labeled 1733.

Also, as implied by the various Latin names, several different but closely related varieties of this rose may have arrived in Europe during a relatively short period of time. Therefore, no one can be certain which of the current cultivars is actually the original 'Slater's Crimson China'.

'*Archduke Charles*' is a 5- or 6-foot-tall , 4- or 5-foot-wide leafy shrub rose with small clusters of large,

'Archduke Charles'

'Green Rose'

double deep pink or crimson flowers that are rimmed attractively with blush pink. Equally suited as an accent shrub and as a deciduous hedge, it was developed about 1837 by a French breeder.

'*Cramoisi Supérieur*' (meaning "superior crimson"), also known as 'Agrippina', is believed to have been developed in France by Coquereau in 1832. It's a rounded, twiggy shrub, 5 feet tall and wide, with small clusters of double 2-inch, crimson blooms. In several respects, it, too, is very much like early descriptions of 'Slater's Crimson China', but it's confused more-often with 'Louis Philippe'.

'Cramoisi Supérieur'

'*Green Rose*' (*Rosa chinensis* var. *viridiflora*) is one of the oddities of the rose world and one which some insist is best suited to collections. It forms a rounded, twiggy, 4- or 5-foot shrub with double, emerald green

"flowers" that last on the plant for weeks and slowly develop a coppery tone. They have a spicy pepper fragrance, typical of the sepals and even the foliage of most china roses. But these aren't flowers; they're actually long-lasting beds of green sepals, with no true petals at all. Known since 1843 and believed to be a sport of 'Old Blush', "Greenie" is either loved or detested by gardeners, without much middle ground. But floral designers seem to universally love it.

'*Mutabilis*' (*Rosa chinensis* var. *mutabilis*), also known as the "Butterfly Bush," is an even-larger shrub yet, growing to be fully 8 feet tall and wide. Its medium-size single flowers open up a pale yellow and then

'Mutabilis'

darken slowly to a deep rose-pink. Consequently, at any one time, it appears to be covered with a mass of multicolored butterflies. It was developed or discovered prior to 1894.

'Old Blush' is still the best-known and most widely grown china rose. It makes an urn-shaped, twiggy shrub, growing from 4 to 8 feet tall, depending on the

'Chi Long Han Zhu'

'Old Blush'

climate. And with a mild winter, it's evergreen, or almost so. It's very resistant to fungal diseases and has very lightly scented, medium-size semidouble flowers in rich pink. One of the first roses to bloom in the spring, 'Old Blush' reblooms in regular flushes until a hard freeze stops it. This habit makes it easy to understand why it's said to be the subject of Thomas Moore's poem, *The Last Rose of Summer*.

'Sanguinea' is a disease-resistant, 3- or 4-foot-tall-and-wide twiggy shrub with small, bright red, fully double, scentless flowers. It's sometimes confused with 'Miss Lowe', which is a smaller, 2-foot shrub with single flowers. 'Chi Long Han Zhu', which has also been called "Willmott's Crimson China," is a closely related variety, about 18 inches tall.

Interestingly, with the exception of 'Miss Lowe', these roses all tend to have fully double flowers in cooler weather. But, in hot weather, they lose petals and become semidouble or even single. And the blood red flowers, especially the single ones, have a distinctive white eye, which is why at least one of them is known in China as "Pearl in Red Dragon's Mouth."

Tea Roses

Description. Unfortunately, like the china roses, the tea roses, as a class, are somewhat cold tender and can only be grown confidently where the winter temperature does not drop below 10°F. But on the positive side, they don't mind summer heat and are some of the most dependable roses for gardeners in Zones 8, 9, and 10.

Shrub-type tea roses—there are a few climbers— tend to be fairly large plants, generally 5 or 6 feet tall and at least that wide. They're disease resistant, but they also require a lot of sun and resent frequent, heavy pruning. Hence, they make excellent, carefree stand-alone, or accent, plants. Tea roses flower all season in a series of flushes, and a few are almost evergreen in mild winters. However, with only a few exceptions, they have rather short and weak flower stems, and their blossoms tend to droop, both on the plant and in flower arrangements.

History. In 1809, a ship arrived from the Orient with a load of tea. Also on board were specimens of a lovely repeat-flowering rose with large and fragrant, double pale pink flowers. Because its fragrance was likened to that of dried tea leaves, it became known as 'Hume's Blush Tea-Scented China'. Even today, some gardeners swear that its fragrance resembles that of a newly opened package of tea.

Certainly, a distinctively sweet, characteristic aroma is associated with tea roses, but few gardeners notice any resemblance to the aroma of tea.

But there's little doubt that these new plants had a tea-like fragrance when they first arrived in England. After all, they'd been stowed with a cargo of tea for several weeks, if not for several months. (It's a blessing that they hadn't sailed the seas with a load of dried codfish.)

'Hume's Blush Tea-Scented China', now considered to be a cultivar of *Rosa* x *odorata*, was followed 15 years later, in 1824, by 'Park's Yellow Tea-Scented China', or *R. odorata* var. *ochroleuca*. Both of these roses are still around today, although both were believed to be lost for a time. They're almost certainly two ancient Chinese garden roses that resulted from either natural or cultivated crosses of the twiggy, repeat-flowering china roses with the wild *Rosa gigantea*.

Crossed with bourbons, noisettes, chinas, and the old European garden roses, these original tea-scented roses ultimately became the parents of a large and wonderful class of shrubby tea roses, developed mostly from the middle to the latter part of the nineteenth century. They were the grandparents of today's hybrid teas.

'Duchesse de Brabant'

'Duchesse de Brabant' presents copious crops of lovely, fragrant, double shell-pink flowers and is semi-evergreen. It seldom has a problem with black spot or powdery mildew. Like most of the teas, it's a rounded shrub, fully 6 feet tall and wide unless kept to a smaller size by trimming and pruning. This rose was introduced in 1857 by H. B. Bèrnede of Bordeaux, France. Brabant is a province in central Belgium.

It's almost mandatory to mention that 'Duchesse de Brabant' is sometimes known as "Teddy Roosevelt's Rose." The long-standing tale is that 'Duchesse' was his favorite rose, so much so that he insisted on wearing one in his lapel when he went to work each day.

'Madame Lombard' has large fragrant, salmon pink flowers with centers that shade toward carmine. It is a bit more cold tender than most tea roses. It is supposedly an 1878 seedling of 'Madame de Tartas' (the tea parent of many fine roses).

'Madame Lombard'

'Monsieur Tillier', often listed as 'Mons. Tillier', is the highest-rated tea rose ranked by the American Rose Society. It's an 1891 cultivar that was raised by Bernaix, but he failed to disclose or record its parentage. It has

'Monsieur Tillier'

large, fragrant, multihued flowers with mixtures of pale pink, salmon pink, and rose-purple.

'Sombreuil' is a modest, 12-foot climbing tea rose with magnificent creamy white or almost white flowers that many rosarians consider to be among the most beautiful and perfectly formed flowers of all roses. (There's something of an ongoing debate as to whether this rose is actually the original 'Sombreuil', but that's not of any importance to the average gardener.) It has large, wonderfully fragrant, many-petaled, flat-faced flowers that are tinged with pale pink in cooler weather. One of the few climbing tea roses, 'Sombreuil' was raised by Robert of Biarritz, France, as an 1850 seedling of 'Gigantesque', itself a seedling of the original 'Park's Yellow Tea-Scented China' rose.

    'Sombreuil' has the reputation of being somewhat

'Sombreuil'

more cold hardy than other tea roses, and it is absolutely immune to powdery mildew. However, it does get some black spot, which is unfortunate because it doesn't have the lushest foliage in the world. But those small clusters of large, fragrant flowers make it all worthwhile.

Noisettes

Description. All of the noisettes are disease resistant, but being southern roses, they also have one real fault. They're relatively cold tender, with some varieties being borderline hardy even in Zone 7b.

History. John Champneys was a rice grower who lived near Charleston, South Carolina, at the beginning of the nineteenth century. His hobby was growing and breeding roses. So, sometime around 1802, he took some pollen from a *Rosa moschata* (the musk rose) and dusted it on his *R. chinensis* ('Old Blush'). The result was an unassuming, 10-foot climber with clusters of small, fragrant, light pink flowers. He dubbed his new rose *R. moschata* var. *hybrida*, a name that was resurrected a hundred years later, anglicized to "hybrid musk," and applied to an entirely different class of roses.

Meanwhile, William Prince, Jr., was the proprietor of the Linnaean Botanic Garden in Flushing, New York, which was at the time America's oldest commercial nursery, having been established in 1737 by William's grandfather. Champneys had dealt previously with this firm, so he proudly sent Prince two tubs of rooted cuttings of his new rose.

Prince was impressed enough to name it 'Champneys' Pink Cluster' and include it in his catalog of 176 varieties of roses. He began shipping it to both his American and European customers in 1811, the year that is generally accepted as the rose's official date of introduction.

Philippe Noisette, a nurseryman of French extraction in Charleston, was a friend of John Champneys. He raised a seedling from a plant Champneys had given him and sent cuttings on to his brother, Louis, a nurseryman and grower near Paris. Louis tagged these roses "Les Rosiers de Philippe Noisette" (meaning "Philippe Noisette's rose bushes"), but we know this variety today as 'Blush Noisette', with a date of introduction of 1817. Then, in 1821, Redouté painted this rose as *Rosa noisettiana*.

Thus were born the noisette roses, the first and only official class of roses to be developed in the United States. Sadly, the man responsible, John Champneys, is remembered and celebrated only by the name of the original variety, 'Champneys' Pink Cluster'.

Noisette roses have figured prominently in the development of other, even better-known roses and classes of roses. Several noisette varieties resulted from crosses with the original tea-scented chinas. Noisettes, crossed with those and with bourbons, resulted in many of the tea roses. Mixed with bourbons, portlands and hybrid chinas, they gave us the hybrid perpetuals. And crosses made with *Rosa multiflora* hybrids resulted in the hybrid musks, which are still referred to as noisettes in parts of Europe.

Noisettes are southern roses and were planted throughout the American South and West during much of the nineteenth and early twentieth centuries. Thus, even today, desirable old noisettes are being rediscovered around old homesteads and in pioneer cemeteries, and placed back on the market.

'Blush Noisette'

'Blush Noisette' is a lovely, lushly foliated, semievergreen, tall shrub or 8- to 9-foot climber. From early spring until the first hard freeze, it produces a continuous display of both small and large clusters of 1½-inch, double, fragrant blush pink flowers. Furthermore, with plenty of sunshine and good cultural practices, it never requires spraying for fungal diseases.

'Céline Forestier' is a noisette with an even more confused background. Some sources say that this rose, with small clusters of light

'Céline Forestier'

rose will grow to 20 feet or more, develop a trunk like a small tree, and present repeating crops of very fragrant large double white to pale pink flowers.

'Maréchal Niel' was a seedling of 'Chromatella', which was a pale yellow seedling of 'Lamarque'. It was introduced by Henry Pradel of Lyon Rhône in 1864 and arrived in this country soon thereafter. Almost immediately, it was adorning arbors, trellises, and porch railings throughout the South. 'Maréchal Niel' has light to medium yellow fragrant nodding flowers

yellow fragrant double flowers, grows to be only 6 feet tall, and was developed in 1858 by a French grower named Leroy. But other sources claim it grows to 16 feet and was developed by Victor Trouillard of Angers, France, in 1842. The latter size is more realistic, but one of the better-known purveyors of old roses takes the easy way out, with a catalog listing that says "6 to 15 feet." On the other hand, it may be that more than one variety of rose is grown under this name. Stranger things have happened.

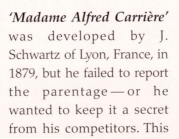

'Madame Alfred Carrière'

'Madame Alfred Carrière' was developed by J. Schwartz of Lyon, France, in 1879, but he failed to report the parentage — or he wanted to keep it a secret from his competitors. This

'Maréchal Niel'

that are so full of petals that they tend to ball in wet weather. But those that do open make it all worthwhile. This rose has a reputation for being more cold tender than most noisettes, but that seems to be somewhat of an exaggeration, as is its reputation for blooming itself to death.

Bourbons

Description. Although there are important exceptions, the majority of bourbon roses are long-caned, arching shrubs with large, full and fragrant flowers. All of them are susceptible to black spot, but some are reasonably tolerant of its attacks and can be grown with only a modicum of attention. Most bourbons are cold hardy to 0°F without protection and will flower repeatedly in the cooler regions. Unfortunately, though, most of them struggle to reflower in the hot summer regions of Zones 8, 9, and 10. They just don't like hot summers coupled with mild winters.

The chief exceptions to this are the lower growing, tea-like shrubs, such as 'Souvenir de la Malmaison' and 'Kronprinzessin Viktoria', and the climber, 'Zéphirine Drouhin'. These all flower reasonably well, even in warmer climates. They're also relatively disease resistant, but they're also more cold tender and may need protection when they are exposed to sustained temperatures below 10°F.

History. Réunion Island is a nondescript speck of land in the western Indian Ocean, about 550 miles east of the island of Madagascar. In the early part of the nineteenth century, it was called the *Île de Bourbon* for the Bourbon kings of France. And it played a large part in the history of old garden roses.

About 1817, two roses on the island engaged in a little hanky-panky, assisted perhaps by a peripatetic bee. A seedling sprouted, was given the name 'Rose Édouard', and grew there for four or five years. Then, seeds of this rose were sent to France and planted in the garden of King Louis-Philippe. From those seeds came a rose, 'Rosier de l'Île de Bourbon' (meaning "Bourbon Island rose bush"). It was distributed in France in 1823 and sent on to England from Paris in 1825 by Louis Noisette.

Thus was initiated a new class of roses that are known today as the bourbon roses. As early as 1838, one excited grower predicted that bourbons would quickly become the most popular of all garden roses.

It's generally accepted that the two roses that begot the first bourbon rose were 'Old Blush' and an autumn damask, most likely 'Quatre Saisons', because these two roses were both found growing as hedges on the island. However, it's also possible—and some believe it to be true—that the autumn damask was actually another "Quatre Saisons" of that time (and this), the carmine-pink 'Tous-les-Mois' (or "every month"), dating from about 1680.

It's generally believed that the rose grown today as 'Rose Édouard' is indeed a clone of the original bourbon rose, even though it was found growing in a garden in India, rather than on Réunion Island.

'Boule de Neige' (meaning "snowball") is another long-caned bourbon of note. François Lacharme of Lyon Rhône developed this rose in 1864 by dusting

'Boule de Neige'

another bourbon, 'Blanche Lafitte', with pollen from 'Sappho', a tea rose grown by Vibert.

'Boule de Neige' has small clusters of medium-size white flowers with petals that reflex until the blooms truly begin to take on the appearance of snowballs. It grows to a height of about 6 feet, is relatively disease resistant, and reblooms fairly well even in warmer climates of Zones 8, 9, and 10.

'Louise Odier' was raised by Jacques-Julien Margottin in Bourg-la-Reine, France, and was introduced in 1851. Another long-caned bourbon, it grows to a height of 5 or 6 feet and has small clusters of strongly fragrant, cupped double flowers in a rich pink.

'Madame Isaac Pereire' is perhaps the most well known of the long-caned bourbons. The chief reason for this is the strong, sweet fragrance of its flowers, an intoxicating blend of damask mixed with just a hint of fresh fruit. Introduced by Garçon of Rouen-Seine,

'Louise Odier'

'Madame Isaac Pereire'

France, in 1881, this rose has large, very double dark pink flowers on limber canes that can grow to a length of 6 or 8 feet. It can be grown as a large, arching shrub. Or, like any of the long-caned bourbons, it can be pegged to make a low, floriferous circle with a diameter of 10 or 12 feet.

'Zéphirine Drouhin' is a 12-to-15-foot climber with large, double, fragrant dark pink to cerise flowers. It's famed for being thornless, a trait that Hercule Poirot used to trap the murderous Nurse Hopkins in Agatha Christie's *Sad Cypress*. And it's one of the more cold hardy climbing roses, tolerating temperatures in Zone 6b with little or no protection. But 'Zéphirine Drouhin' can be grown successfully in Zone 5 if the crown is protected with a thick mound of soil or mulch.

'Zéphirine Drouhin'

Hybrid Perpetuals

Description. Hybrid perpetuals are quite cold hardy and can be grown with a little protection in Zone 5b. But most of them have some susceptibility to powdery mildew, black spot, and other fungal diseases. Thus, it's a stretch to label them as easy-care roses. On the other hand, their vigor, nostalgic flower forms, and usefulness as bold accent plants can make any extra effort worthwhile.

Most hybrid perpetuals have long, stiff canes with stout prickles and sparse greenery. Flowers tend to be large and double, and most of them have at least some fragrance. They bloom at the ends of the canes in small clusters, with the flowers of many cultivars snuggled into the leaves much like the portland roses. Their colors range from pure white and light pink to deep rose and dark red, with only the yellows entirely absent from their palettes.

When pegged, a hybrid perpetual will break all along the canes, thereby yielding more flowers. So, just as with the long-caned bourbons, many of them are grown best in this manner. Otherwise, the taller ones can actually be grown as small climbers.

History. Hybrid perpetuals evolved from attempts to combine the best qualities of the gallicas, portlands, and bourbons—their flower size, form, and fragrance—with the repeat-flowering attributes of the china roses. The early results were strongly reminiscent of the bourbons, with their full-bodied, very double, intoxicatingly fragrant flowers. But as time progressed, growers developed an obsession with flower form, the same fixation that was to afflict so many growers during the second half of the twentieth century.

They concentrated on developing exhibition-quality, brightly colored flowers on long, stiff stems, while ignoring overall form, vigor, and flower fragrance. As a result, many of the hybrid perpetuals that appeared near the end of the nineteenth century have flowers with a form that closely resembles that of the modern hybrid tea roses.

Jean Laffay was as responsible as any one grower could be for the early development and evolution of the hybrid perpetuals. Using chinas, bourbons, and portlands, he created a series of repeat-blooming roses he termed Hybrides Remontants. His first successful variety was 'Princesse Hélene', which he introduced in 1837. Unfortunately, this historic rose appears to be lost from commerce—at least by that name.

"Hybrid Perpetual" is a translation of Laffay's French label. "Remontant" infers a repeat bloom, mainly in the fall and with fewer blossoms the second time around. "Perpetual" is misleading, however. But some of them repeat quite well, especially in regions with warm, balmy days and cool nights.

By the end of the nineteenth century, at least 2,500 hybrid perpetuals had been introduced. Today, less than 200 still exist in commerce. These are grandmother's "old cabbage roses," the varieties that bloomed the best, exhibited reasonable disease resistance, and had some of the higher-quality flowers.

'Baronne Prévost' was developed in 1842 by Jean Desprez in Yèbels, France, and is one of the more floriferous hybrid perpetuals. Tall and erect, with a

'Baronne Prévost'

height of 5 or 6 feet and a width of 3 or 4 feet, it has large, very double, flat-faced, strongly fragrant rich pink flowers that resemble bourbon roses. It's one of the more cold-hardy, yet heat-tolerant hybrid perpetuals and, in some regions, has the added reputation of being relatively resistant to black spot and powdery mildew.

'La Reine' (meaning "the queen") is of unknown parentage, but it was introduced in France by Laffay in 1842. It's a sun-loving, erect shrub, 4 to 6 feet tall,

'Marchessa Boccella'

'La Reine'

which flowers regularly in all but the hottest and driest parts of a summer. It has large, cupped, very double, rich pink flowers with a strong, sweet fragrance. And it's not quite as susceptible to black spot and other fungal diseases as are some of the hybrid perpetuals.

'Marchessa Boccella' ('Marquise de Boccella') has been confused almost beyond any hope of reclamation with the portland rose, 'Jacques Cartier'. And yet it's one of the highest rated and most popular of all hybrid perpetuals. Developed by Desprez in 1842, it has medium-size, fully double, pompon-shaped, clear pink flowers on an upright, long-caned, shrub only 4 or 5 feet tall and 3 or 4 feet wide. They are fragrant.

'Reine des Violettes' ("queen of the violets"), developed in 1860 by Millet-Malet, is another upright, well-branched, mostly thornless shrub. It blooms well with small, double, pleasantly fragrant soft violet-pink flowers.

'Reine des Violettes'

Hybrid Teas

Description. Most hybrid teas are upright, urn-shaped bushes, 3 to 5 feet tall, with stiff, thorny canes that tend to become "bare-legged" with age. They bloom singly or in small clusters, with a flush of flowers every five or six weeks throughout the season. They vary considerably in their resistance to fungal diseases: those with yellow and yellow-pink flowers generally being the most susceptible. Most hybrid teas can withstand winter temperatures down to –10°F (Zone 6a) with only moderate protection.

In the hotter regions of Zones 8, 9, and 10, gardeners often find that some modern hybrid teas will struggle to survive in the garden. And they don't flower well at all after that first flush in the year they're planted. If this is your experience or situation, there is a simple solution. Grow your rose in a container. You can grow any hybrid tea in a deep 14-inch-diameter container for five or six years before it needs re-potting. And it will flower better and remain healthier than its brothers and sisters out in the garden.

History. Officially, the era of modern roses began with the introduction of the very first hybrid tea. Furthermore, because all the early hybrid teas were created by crossing hybrid perpetuals with tea roses, it is commonly believed that the name "hybrid tea" is a composite of "hybrid" from hybrid perpetual and "tea" from the second parent. But neither of these notions is entirely correct.

It's true that 'La France' has long been designated officially as the original hybrid tea, but that may not have been actually the case. Still, because 'La France' was introduced in 1867, that year is the official demarcation line between classes of old garden roses and modern roses.

'La France' was introduced by Jean-Baptiste Guillot fils of Lyon, France. Some reports say that he dusted flowers of 'Madame Victor Verdier', an 1863 hybrid perpetual, with pollen from his 1846 tea rose, 'Madame

Bravy'. But this parentage is not totally accepted, probably because Guillot fils, himself, stated that 'La France' was a seedling of his own 1858 tea rose, 'Madame Falcot'.

According to the rule that requires a rose to be assigned to the class of its seed parent, the first parentage would make 'La France' a hybrid perpetual; the second would make it a tea rose. So it would be nice to know which lineage is correct, even though it no longer matters.

In any case, 'La France' wasn't designated as a "hybrid tea" until more than a decade after its introduction. And even now some believe that 'Madame Falcot' is more deserving of the honor of being the first hybrid tea.

Actually, Henry Bennett of Salisbury, England, developed the first roses to be dubbed with the sobriquet "hybrid tea." In 1879, after conducting a series of scientifically designed crosses of teas with hybrid perpetuals, he introduced ten new varieties he called "Pedigree Hybrids of the Tea Rose." The Horticultural Society of Lyon, France, after listening to Bennett lecture about his carefully constructed experiments the following year, decided to call these roses *Hybrides de Thé*, which translates as "tea hybrids" or "hybrid teas." And thus the name of the class was born.

Only after scouring the records for similar crosses of earlier roses did the moguls of the rose world finally agree to designate 'La France' as the first hybrid tea and as the prototype for its class. And it's difficult to argue with their choice, for 'La France' has the classic bud and flower form that has come to be associated with all the best varieties of hybrid teas. About its only drawback is that it still has some of the weak-neck syndrome of its tea-rose parent.

'La France' is also one of those unfair ironies of history. Guillot fils is credited with its development and introduction, and it's celebrated officially as the first hybrid tea. But even though it's generally agreed that Henry Bennett was the creator of the class, his name doesn't appear in any list of hybrid tea roses. At least John Champneys, creator of the first noisette rose, is remembered with 'Champneys' Pink Cluster.' Perhaps it would be appropriate for someone to name a new hybrid tea "Souvenir de Henry Bennett."

Of the more than 13,000 varieties of roses known to be in commerce today, it's likely that well over 50 percent are hybrid teas. But they didn't rise to such dominance until 'Peace' was formally introduced at the end of World War II. Still, many classic and historically important cultivars were developed in the period between 1867 and 1945. And many more excellent cultivars have been developed since then. Here are only a few of the many classic and worthwhile hybrid teas from these two eras, with the arrival of 'Peace' as the demarcation between them.

'Antoine Rivoire' was cherished for many years as a rose for cutting, both in the garden and at the florist shop. Introduced in 1895 by Joseph Pernet of the firm of Pernet-Ducher of Lyon, France, this vigorous grower was a son of the 1886 tea rose, 'Dr. Grill', crossed with 'Lady Mary Fitzwilliam'. It's another famous parent of many modern hybrid teas and has mildly fragrant, double pale pink-blend flowers on a tall, upright bush.

'Peace' has been the all-time best-known, best-loved, and best-selling hybrid tea, almost from the moment of its introduction.

'Peace' has charming, double, large, and mildly fragrant flowers that are an ever-changing blend of

'Peace'

yellow, pink, and carmine. But its vigor is also a throwback to its antique-rose ancestors. Given a full day of sun and not pruned severely each year, 'Peace' will form a large, handsome shrub, fully 7 feet tall and 4 feet wide, well-foliated, and almost always in bloom to some extent. It has an unfortunate susceptibility to black spot but never seems to suffer any long-lasting damage from it.

Oddly, though, its parentage isn't certain. What is certain is that it was developed in 1935 by Francis Meilland, and that he named it 'Madame Antoine

'Antoine Rivoire'

Meilland' in honor of his mother, Claudia. Then, at the end of World War II and upon the inauguration of the United Nations, it was renamed 'Peace'.

The era of truly modern hybrid teas began with 'Peace'. And hybridizers have worked ever since to create new varieties that would meet the standards set by that rose. Unfortunately, until near the end of the twentieth century, they concentrated almost entirely on flower form and color, ignoring fragrance, disease resistance, and overall vigor. As a result, many beautiful, but disease-prone varieties were offered for sale. And for a time, only a small percentage of them had any significant fragrance.

Still, a number of vigorous, disease-resistant, and fragrant varieties were introduced during the last half of the twentieth century. And with customers showing a renewed interest in these attributes, growers appear to be producing more each and every year. On the other hand, a truly definitive judgment cannot be made until a variety has been grown for several years. So each new hybrid tea, if it's to stay around, must meet the test of time.

'Double Delight' was developed by Swim and Ellis and introduced by the Armstrong Nursery of Ontario, California, in 1977. It has won almost every rose prize in

'Double Delight'

existence and was voted the world's most popular rose in 1985. A robust, shrubby plant that grows 4 or 5 feet tall, it has charming, double, very fragrant flowers that open a creamy white and quickly become a blend of white and strawberry red. On the down side, it's susceptible to powdery mildew, and it resents spraying.

'First Prize', developed by E. S. Boerner and introduced by Jackson & Perkins of Medford, Oregon, in 1970, is a vigorous, upright, disease-resistant plant with impressively thorny canes. This prize-winning

'First Prize'

rose has very large double flowers that are a lovely blend of muted rose-pink and ivory.

'Fragrant Cloud' was developed by Math Tantau in Germany in 1963 and introduced in North America by Jackson & Perkins in 1968. This vigorous, erect bush, which reaches a height of 4 or 5 feet tall and spreads 3 feet, has large semidouble flowers that open a coral-red and begin to change to more of a geranium red after a day or two.

It has some susceptibility to black spot but will be excused for that shortcoming by anyone who enjoys fragrant roses. True to its name, 'Fragrant Cloud' won the prestigious James Alexander Gamble Rose

'Fragrant Cloud'

Fragrance Award in 1970. And in 1981 it was named the world's favorite rose.

'Mister Lincoln' was developed by Swim & Weeks and introduced in 1964 by Conard-Pyle. An upright shrub that grows easily to a height of 6 feet and a

'Mister Lincoln'

width of 3 feet, this classic rose has large and double, extremely fragrant dark red flowers. Its only real faults are a susceptibility to powdery mildew and a general dislike for cool, damp climates.

'Olympiad' is a classic deep-red exhibition rose. But being quite disease resistant, it's also a wonderful

garden rose, although its flowers have little or no fragrance. It's an upright bush, growing to 4 feet tall and 2 feet wide, with large, slightly double flowers

'Olympiad'

borne singly on long stems. 'Olympiad' was developed by McGredy Roses and introduced in 1984 in Los Angeles in connection with the inauguration of the Olympic Games.

'Touch of Class', also known as 'Maréchal le Clerc', was developed by Michel Kriloff of Antibes, France, and introduced in North America in 1984 by the Armstrong Nursery of California. This classic exhibition and cutting rose has large, double, high-centered, mildly fragrant, coral to creamy pink flowers. It's generally disease resistant but will occasionally be attacked by powdery mildew.

'Touch of Class'

A Tale of Peace

In the spring of 1935, Antoine Meilland and his son, Francis, selected the 50 most promising rose seedlings from the 800 crosses they had made that year. Then, in 1936, the 50 survivors were budded onto sturdy rootstocks, replanted, and grown on for further trial.

In June, 1939, an international conference of rose hybridizers was held in Lyon, near the Meilland rose fields. Papa Meilland and Francis took advantage of the occasion to invite their customers to inspect their new crop of roses.

The international guests gathered around seedling 3-35-40, one of the 50 plants chosen for further trial in 1935. The rose enthusiasts marveled at this elegant rose, with its long-stemmed buds slowly opening to display an abundance of petals, brushed with soft pink over a blend of ivory and pale gold.

By September of that year, France was already technically at war with Germany. Not knowing what might lie ahead, Francis Meilland did what he could to preserve his wonderful new rose. He sent small bundles of bud wood to growers he knew in Turkey, Italy, and Germany. And at the last minute he managed to have a fourth package hand-carried by the American consul to his friend Robert Pyle of the Conard-Pyle Company in the United States.

The carefully packaged bud wood never made it to Turkey. The German army invaded Yugoslavia while it was in transit. The Germans threw out all the passengers and all the mail when they confiscated the trains.

But Meilland's packages arrived safely in Italy and in Germany. When the rose flowered, the Italian grower took one look and named it 'Gioia', which translates as "Joy." The German grower was equally enthralled; he named the rose 'Gloria Dei', or "Glory of God".

Meilland was unaware of these events. All during the long years of war, he could only wait and wonder if any of his packages had gotten through. Meanwhile, he continued to propagate 3-35-40 and ultimately named it 'Madame A. Meilland' in memory of his mother, Claudia. He used that form of her name because that was how Papa Meilland had addressed his letters to her during World War I.

Finally, in 1944, exactly one month after the liberation of France, Meilland received a letter from Robert Pyle. "While dictating this letter," it said, "my eyes are fixed in fascinated admiration on a glorious rose, its pale gold, cream, and ivory petals blending to a lightly ruffled edge of delicate carmine. I am convinced this will be the greatest rose of the century."

Pyle's letter explained that he had propagated 3-35-40 and sent specimens to other growers around the country to test. Pyle wrote that the American Rose Society wanted to hold a name-giving ceremony for this wonderful new rose at the Pacific Rose Society's Annual Exhibition to be held in California, on April 29, 1945. Pyle wanted Meilland's approval of the name, 'Peace'.

And so it was that 'Peace' was formally introduced in the United States in 1945. But it was introduced to the world four days earlier. When delegates gathered for the inaugural meeting of the United Nations on April 25, a bud vase with a single long-stemmed 'Peace' rose was waiting in each of their hotel rooms.

Since those historic days, 'Peace' has won almost every prize and medal awarded in the rose world. And Pyle's predictions that it would become the "Rose of the Twentieth Century" came true. 'Peace' not only set a new standard for roses, but it is, far and away, the best-selling rose of all time. And all because Papa Meilland decided it was worthy of including with those 49 other little seedlings on that fateful day in 1935.

Polyanthas

Description. Polyanthas present clusters of diminutive, colorful, mostly scentless flowers on small- to medium-size leafy shrubs ideal for containers, as border plants, and as shrubs in small landscapes. But not all polyanthas fit this description or these uses. A few varieties are relatively large shrubs, 6 feet or more tall. And there are a few climbers as well.

Rugged and vigorous, polyanthas demonstrate a reasonable amount of resistance to insect pests and diseases. They're generally heat tolerant, and can withstand winter temperatures down to 0°F—and even lower with a little protection. So they can be grown readily throughout most of climate Zones 6 through 10, where they'll bloom repeatedly from late spring into fall or early winter.

History. During the last half of the nineteenth century, gardeners began to lust after relatively small shrub roses that would present masses of color over a long season. And the form of the flowers was not nearly so important as before. This demand inspired the creation of a new class of roses that, for a while, were even more popular than the newly developing hybrid teas.

Around 1860, Guillot fils received the seeds of a white-flowering form of *R. multiflora* from a plant hunter in Japan. He raised the seedlings and pollinated them with flowers from a dwarf form of *R. chinensis*, but he got only once-flowering offspring. Undaunted, he proceeded with his experiment and was rewarded handsomely when the second generation produced two repeat-flowering dwarf shrub roses only 18 to 20 inches tall and wide.

One of these new hybrids produced clusters of 40 white, 1-inch flowers. Guillot fils named it 'Ma Pâquerette' (meaning "my daisy") and introduced it in 1875. The other cultivar he held off the market until 1880. Named 'Mignonette' (more or less "cutie pie"), it bore even larger clusters of as many as 50 small pink and white flowers.

Guillot fils decided to call his new roses polypoms because he thought the flower clusters resembled little pom-poms. Today, these roses are known as polyanthas, the Greek term for many flowers.

Once 'Ma Pâquerette' and 'Mignonette' had been released in the market, rose breeders throughout Europe began working to create similar cultivars. Then, just a short time later, they began mixing in other species roses, tea roses, and even some noisettes and hybrid teas. Eventually this resulted in larger shrubs with larger flowers that were, at first, called hybrid polyanthas and, then, floribundas, the name they're known by today. A sizable number of polyantha roses are still being grown today, 'Ma Pâquerette' (as simply 'Pâquerette') and 'Mignonette' among them.

'Cécile Brunner', also known as 'Mignon', is probably most famous as grandmother's old 'Sweetheart Rose'. Three forms are available: a small 3-foot shrub rose; a 6-foot so-called "spray" rose; and a vigorous, 25-foot

'Cécile Brunner'

climbing rose. All three versions are almost thornless and have identical 1-inch, mildly fragrant flowers in light pink with the high-centered form of a modern hybrid tea blossom. They have good disease resistance and are in flower almost continuously after becoming established.

Ducher of Lyon-Rhône, France, developed the original shrub form in 1881. The spray form, a taller and larger sport of the original, was introduced in 1919. And the climbing sport has appeared twice, first in 1894 and then again in 1904.

It's well to note that, contrary to many reports, the spray form of this rose is a true sport of the original 'Cécile Brunner' and not the floribunda rose introduced in 1920 as 'Bloomfield Abundance'. That rose, which evidently resembled 'Cécile Brunner' in some respects, has apparently been lost.

'China Doll' was developed in 1946 by Dr. W. E. Lammerts of Livermore, California. 'China Doll' is a dwarf 1½-foot-tall shrub with an almost continuous

'China Doll'

display of semidouble, 1- to 2-inch, lightly fragrant, rose pink flowers in large clusters. A climbing sport also exists, but it doesn't flower nearly as well as the shrub form.

'Marie Pavié' (also listed as 'Marie Parvie') is a 3-foot, almost thornless shrub introduced by Alégatière of Lyon, France, in 1888. Despite some susceptibility to

'Marie Pavié'

black spot, this rose flowers repeatedly, with small clusters of mildly fragrant, double 2-inch flowers in blush white.

'Phyllis Bide' is a climbing polyantha that grows to a height of 8 to 10 feet and is ideal for a pillar or for a small arbor or trellis. It was introduced in 1923 by Bide

'Phyllis Bide'

& Sons of Farnham, England, and blooms repeatedly and profusely with loose clusters of small, mildly fragrant, semidouble flowers that are a charming blend of golden yellow and pale pink.

'The Fairy', introduced in 1932 by Bentall of Havering-Romford, England, may well be the best-known and best-loved of all the polyantha roses. A thickly foliated, very prickly shrub, 1½ feet to 2 feet tall

'The Fairy'

and 3 feet wide, it blooms repeatedly with tight clusters of small, rich pink scentless flowers that can bleach to an eggshell white under an August sun. Otherwise heat tolerant and disease-free, it's popular for use as a low-growing hedge, as a bed edging or border, and as a showy plant for large containers.

Hybrid Rugosas

Description. Rugosa roses, sometimes known as Japanese roses, are native to the near-shore areas of northeastern China, Korea, and Japan, where winters are fierce indeed. Consequently, they can withstand temperatures of –40°F. Rugosas actually prefer light, sandy soils and tolerate salt air well. They are immune or extremely resistant to black spot and powdery mildew.

At the same time, the rugosas and many of the hybrid rugosas also have other qualities that you should consider before planting one in the garden with your other roses. They resent being sprayed with pesticides or fungicides of any kind, they don't really enjoy being heavily fertilized, and most of them won't do well at all in Zones 9 and 10, especially along the humid Gulf Coast. They can be difficult to grow successfully in the hotter regions of Zone 8.

History. The original rugosa roses apparently arrived in Europe sometime in the late 1700s, but nobody paid much attention to them. They didn't offer anything new for the gardeners of that time, their shapeless single blossoms weren't really suitable for use as cut flowers, and their prickly and uncouth appearance didn't compare favorably with that of the existing shrub-type roses.

By the end of the nineteenth century, though, people began to recognize the peculiar attributes of rugosa roses—that is, their extreme cold hardiness and disease resistance. And they soon found that rugosas could be crossed with just about any other type of rose

Hips of R. rugosa

duced from time to time. Also, because of their cold hardiness and disease resistance, they're the patriarchs of several types of modern shrub roses that have been developed primarily for use in colder parts of the country and for regions where fungal diseases run rampant.

to yield an attractive and worthwhile shrub. Those hybrids almost invariably retained the cold hardiness and at least some of the disease resistance of the rugosa clan.

Today, there are many hybrid rugosa roses from which to choose in addition to the two sports of the original species rose, *Rosa rugosa* var. *rubra* and *R. rugosa* var. *alba*. And new hybrids are still being intro-

R. rugosa *var.* alba

R. rugosa var. rubra is believed to be a sport of the original species rose and was probably introduced into Europe at about the same time. It's a large, rounded shrub that can grow up to 6 feet tall and wide. Like all rugosas, its leaflets are heavily veined and ridged—rugosa means "rough or wrinkled." And they're a handsome dark green that turns a golden yellow in autumn. But its canes are extremely prickly. It blooms regularly all season, and its large, loosely formed flowers are single (five petaled), a deep rose purple, and very fragrant. Appearing in small clusters, they have a pleasant clove-like scent. Unless deadheaded, the flowers are followed by large and nutritious, globe-shaped, cherry red hips. And deadheading doesn't seem to increase flowering to any great extent.

R. rugosa var. alba is also believed to be a sport of the original species rose. It's like *R. rugosa* var. *rubra* in all respects, except that its flowers are a pristine white.

R. rugosa

'Belle Poitevine' was one of the early hybrid rugosas, having been introduced in 1894 by Bruant of Portiers, France. It forms a dense, rounded, 5-foot, repeat-flow-

'Belle Poitevine'

ering shrub with large, fragrant, semidouble flowers that are a pleasant rose-pink. And it usually sets a few large scarlet hips.

'Frau Dagmar Hastrup', often listed mistakenly as 'Frau Dagmar Hartopp', was introduced by Hastrup in

'Frau Dagmar Hastrup'

Denmark in 1914. It has small clusters of large, single, fragrant pale pink flowers on a dense, rounded, 4-foot shrub. And it sets crops of hips that look like large maraschino cherries.

'Henry Hudson' is a hybrid rugosa from the Explorer Series. It was introduced in 1976 by Agriculture Canada and has medium-size, cupped, semidouble

'Henry Hudson'

fragrant white flowers on an upright shrub, 3 or 4 feet tall. It's one of the hardiest of the series, but it isn't self-cleaning, so you need to deadhead it regularly to maintain a neat appearance.

'Schneezwerg' (meaning "snow dwarf") has small clusters of 2½-inch, semidouble, fragrant pure white flowers, followed by occasional hips. This relatively small shrub, only 3 or 4 feet tall and wide, was used by Dr. Felicitas Svejda as the seed parent in the development of her cold-hardy and disease-resistant roses that became the first of the Canadian Explorer Series. It's also more tolerant of warm summer areas than are most hybrid rugosas.

'Schneezwerg'

Hybrid Musks

Description. As a general rule, hybrid musk roses can be trimmed and used as 4- or 5-foot shrubs, but they really prefer to be grown as large, arching shrub roses or small climbers. They can be grown in most of the more-temperate parts of the country, tolerating both the summer heat of Zones 8 and 9 and the coldest regions, right up to the fringes of Zone 6b. As a group, they have a reasonably good resistance to fungal diseases and seem never to suffer any serious damage if they are affected with this problem.

Hybrid musks bloom repeatedly, with large clusters of small-to medium-size flowers. And some of them have a delightful old-rose fragrance that, on a warm and humid evening, can perfume an entire garden.

History. The origin of the hybrid musk roses must be credited to two different men, Peter Lambert and the Reverend Joseph Pemberton. Neither has sole claim to their development, and neither could have been successful without the other, although the two men may never have met.

In 1904, Peter Lambert, a nurseryman in Trier, Germany, introduced a rose he had named for his city. This new rose, 'Trier', was a multiflora-noisette cross by way of its seed parent, 'Aglaia', a rose he had introduced previously, in 1896. Today, the American Rose Society classes both of these roses as hybrid multifloras, but they're considered by many to be the first hybrid musk roses, even though that name wasn't used until much later and was quite a stretch even then.

The only association either of these roses had with the wild musk rose is through the noisette branch of their lineage. And to find it there, the line has to be traced all the way back to the original noisette, 'Champneys' Pink Cluster'.

Reverend Joseph Pemberton had been a serious rosarian for many years. So when he retired from his job with the Church of England in 1909, he began breeding roses at his home in Havering-atte-Bower in Essex. With the aim of creating a new line of shrub roses, he began crossing Lambert's 'Aglaia' and 'Trier' with hybrid teas, hybrid perpetuals, and tea roses. His efforts were successful. In 1913, Reverend Pemberton introduced two new roses, 'Danaë' and 'Moonlight'. At first, these roses and the several examples he released during the next few years—including 'Vanity' in 1920 and 'Penelope' in 1924—were known as "Lambertianas" in honor of Peter Lambert. Only later were they renamed hybrid musks, and in Europe they're still sometimes classed as noisettes.

Reverend Pemberton died in 1926, and his sister Florence took over his project, working with Pemberton's gardeners, Joseph and Ann Bentall. Together, the three of them released 'Robin Hood' in 1927 and 'Felicia' in 1928. Finally, the Bentalls started their own nursery and continued the Pemberton family work until the beginning of World War II. Wilhelm Kordes and his son Reimer of Offenseth-Sparrieshoop, Germany, carried on during the war and in the years since.

'Ballerina' was introduced by the Bentalls in 1937. It can be grown as an attractive, rounded shrub, 4 feet

'Ballerina'

tall and wide, or it may be used as a small climber in which case it will reach to a height of as much as 8 or 10 feet. Either way, it's covered early and late with large clusters of small, single pale pink flowers with charming white eyes. Unfortunately, those flowers don't have much fragrance.

'Buff Beauty' is considered by some to be the queen of the hybrid musks. It was released by Ann Bentall in 1939, but is possibly considerably older than that. The

'Buff Beauty'

long, arching canes of this rose develop into a mounded shrub, 6 feet tall and wide. And when grown as a climber, its canes can become at least twice that long. It blooms well throughout the year, with clusters of 3- to 4-inch, very double, sweetly fragrant flowers that are a pleasing blend of yellow, apricot, and coral. It's somewhat prone to black spot in some areas, but this rose never seems to sustain any serious damage.

'Penelope' is a Pemberton-developed rose that was introduced in 1924. It's a tall, bushy, vigorous, disease-free shrub, 5 feet tall and 3 or 4 feet wide, with clusters of sweetly fragrant, 3-inch, semi-

'Penelope'

double, light pink flowers that have a hint of lemon yellow in the centers. After opening, they fade quickly to a blush white and, if left on the plant, will set coral pink hips.

Floribundas and Grandifloras

Description. Floribundas are cluster-flowered roses that evolved slowly during the first half of the twentieth century, as the polyanthas were crossed with hybrid teas and other large-flowered roses.

In general, they're small- to medium-size rounded shrubs with a healthy complement of foliage that, in many varieties, is quite disease resistant. Most floribunda buds bloom open sequentially. Because of this, a cluster can have young buds, ripe buds showing color, freshly opened flowers, fading flowers, and spent flowers, all at the same time.

On the other hand, grandifloras typically have larger flowers on longer stems and in smaller clusters than do the floribundas. And all the buds in a cluster open at about the same time. Grandifloras also tend to be taller, more-upright plants than do the floribundas, and most varieties have high-centered, exhibition-type flowers. All of these characteristics are due to a greater infusion of hybrid tea genes.

Otherwise, the distinction between the two groups is not well-defined. And no doubt, this is the reason *grandiflora* is an official designation only in North America and among a few French rosarians. The rest of the world never adopted the term as a class name and now refers to both floribundas and grandifloras simply as "cluster-flowered" roses.

Floribundas, as a whole, are a little hardier than hybrid teas and can endure, with only a modicum of protection, temperatures down to −10°F, which is into Zone 5b. At the other extreme, several varieties are quite heat tolerant and will perform well even in Zones 9 and 10.

Grandifloras tend to have a cold tolerance similar to that of their floribunda relatives and the loathing for too-high temperatures associated with most of their hybrid tea parents. There are, of course, individual exceptions in both classes.

History. Supposedly, Dr. J. H. Nicolas of the Jackson & Perkins company first suggested, in 1930, the name "floribunda" as a marketing label for the shrubby roses that, up until then, had been tagged mostly as "hybrid polyanthas." Then "grandiflora" came into being in 1954 as a term used to describe 'Queen Elizabeth', which was considered to be the first of another new type of rose. Today, the American Rose Society recognizes these as the names of two classes of similar, but yet different types of roses.

'Betty Prior' was developed by Prior & Son of Colchester, England, and introduced in 1935. This classic floribunda blooms profusely throughout the season,

'Betty Prior'

with large clusters of charming 3-inch, flat-faced, single, slightly fragrant, rich carmine pink flowers on a leafy, upright shrub, 4 to 5 feet tall.

'Bill Warriner' has large clusters of 2-inch, orange-pink flowers on an urn-shaped, 3-foot-tall, 2-foot-wide shrub. It's extremely disease resistant and flowers repeatedly from spring through fall. This rose was developed by Keith Zary of the Jackson & Perkins

'Bill Warriner'

company of Medford, Oregon, and released by that firm in 1996. Bill Warriner, who died in 1991, was a long-time rose breeder with Jackson & Perkins.

'Caribbean' is a vigorous disease-resistant, 5-foot-tall and upright thorny bush with small clusters or sprays of large double fragrant flowers that are a charming

'Caribbean'

blend of apricot-orange and yellow. It was developed by the Kordes firm of Sparrieshoop, Germany, and introduced in 1992.

'Europeana'

'Europeana' was introduced in 1963 by George de Ruiter of Holland. It's a vigorous, rounded, 4-foot-tall, 3-foot-wide shrub that is seldom out of bloom, with large clusters of 3-inch, double, slightly fragrant, carmine-red flowers. It's prone to powdery mildew in humid environments, and will occasionally develop some black spot. Other than that, its only fault is that the flower clusters are sometimes too large and heavy for the stems.

'French Lace' has small clusters of high-centered, double, slightly fragrant flowers that are a pale ivory shading to a light apricot in the center.

This rose, which was developed in 1980 by Bill Warriner of Jackson & Perkins, is a small, 3-foot, bushy

'French Lace'

plant. An excellent cut flower, 'French Lace' is not as cold hardy as most floribundas; it performs best in areas no colder than Zone 7a.

'Iceberg' has long been the most popular of the white floribunda roses. Released in 1958 by Reimer Kordes of Sparrieshoop, Germany, this leafy, upright, 4-foot-tall, 3-foot-wide shrub has repeating clusters of mildly fragrant 3-inch, pure white flowers—except in cool weather when they may be blushed with a hint of pink. 'Iceberg' is essentially immune to powdery mildew but will exhibit a mild susceptibility to black spot in some parts of the country. It blooms well all season and is an excellent cut flower.

'Iceberg'

This rose has a climbing sport with a unique character. Sold as 'Climbing Iceberg,' it flowers every bit as well as the original, a habit rarely encountered among the climbing sports of bush and shrub roses.

'Livin' Easy' is a disease-resistant rose hybridized by Jack Harkness of Hitchin, England, and introduced in 1992. Its medium-size, semidouble, salmon-orange flowers appear on a vigorous, leafy shrub that is 3 or 4 feet tall and wide.

'Livin' Easy'

'Pink Parfait' was developed by Herbert Swim of Ontario, California, and introduced in 1960. During the spring and fall, the large, almost-double flowers are a rich pink, grading to a lighter orange-pink at the centers. But during the hottest part of summer, they're

'Pink Parfait'

a much lighter pink throughout. They have a mild, sweet fragrance and are produced repeatedly in small clusters on an upright, 4-foot-tall, 3-foot-wide bush.

This rose is generally resistant to or relatively tolerant of fungal diseases, but black spot may be a problem in some parts of the country.

'Playboy' (or 'Cheerio') laughs at fungal diseases. Released in 1976 by James Cocker of Scotland, its large, almost single, slightly scented flowers are a pleasing blend of gold, orange, and scarlet and are at

'Queen Elizabeth'

'Playboy'

their very best and brightest in a warm climate. Small flower clusters appear regularly throughout the season on a branching, upright and leafy 3-foot bush.

'Queen Elizabeth' (aka 'The Queen Elizabeth Rose'), voted the World's Favorite Rose in 1979, was developed by Dr. W. E. Lammerts of California, and introduced in 1954. The first grandiflora rose and the archetype for the class, it has small clusters of large, double, high-centered, fragrant rich pink flowers on a shrubby, upright plant, fully 6 feet tall and 3 feet wide.

Its disease resistance, however, is something of an enigma. In many parts of the country, 'Queen Elizabeth' is revered for having few or no problems with fungal diseases.

In other areas, this rose cursed for being susceptible to black spot. Because that is the case, it's possible

that its resistance to black spot is related more to the prevalent strains of fungi than to either climate or weather.

'Sunsprite' was introduced in 1977 by Reimer Kordes of Germany, and won the coveted Gamble fragrance

'Sunsprite'

medal two years later. This disease-free yellow rose presents repeating clusters of large, barely double, rich yellow flowers on a vigorous, upright plant, 3 to 4 feet tall and 2 to 3 feet wide. The flowers are very fragrant.

'Tournament of Roses' was introduced in 1988 to commemorate the 100th anniversary of the New Year's Day parade in Pasadena, California. Developed by Bill

'Tournament of Roses'

Warriner of Jackson & Perkins, this rose is a 6-foot, upright, thorny shrub, with small clusters of large, double, high-centered flowers with little or no fragrance. Their color is a light pink blend, with a darker, richer pink on the reverse.

Shrub Roses

Description. Shrub roses include many of the newer roses bred for disease resistance and cold tolerance rather than for exquisite flower form. This class includes roses that are being developed for use as landscape plants — for hedges or borders and as accent plants — rather than for use primarily in formal beds or as exhibition flowers.

Shrub roses may be plants that are 2 feet tall and a foot wide, or they may be plants that are 10 feet tall and 12 feet wide. They may have small flowers in large clusters, or they may have large blooms on long, straight stems. They may be wonderfully fragrant, or they may have all the aroma of yesterday's newspaper. None of these things count. It's their mixed ancestry and their shrubby character that counts.

History. Technically, all roses are shrubs, and some varieties have been labeled as such for many years, although they were officially assigned to some specific class, such as bourbon, tea, or hybrid musk. Nowadays, though, shrub roses is a formal class of its own. In it are those newer roses that exhibit many of the characteristics of the old roses traditionally referred to as "shrubs," along with all those nonclimbing roses that are such a mixture of ancestry they just do not fit into any other official class.

Leading the way in the development of modern shrub roses have been such luminaries as Griffith Buck and David Austin, as well as firms such as Jackson & Perkins of the United States, Meilland of France, Kordes of Germany, and Poulsen of Denmark.

Griffith Buck Roses

The late Dr. Griffith J. Buck of Iowa State University in Ames, Iowa, developed and released as many as 80 new cultivars that were the results of a program designed to develop roses that were not only very cold hardy, but also highly resistant or even immune to black spot. As a result, most of these roses will tolerate temperatures down to –25°F (Zone 4b) with no protection whatsoever. And, perhaps surprisingly, the Buck shrub roses are also tolerant of heat, flourishing in Zones 8, 9, and 10. As a rule, they're either very resistant to black spot or smugly tolerant of its attacks and seldom, if ever, require treatment of any kind.

'Carefree Beauty' was introduced in 1977 and, throughout the country is one of the most popular of the Buck shrub roses. (In some areas, it—or an almost

'Hawkeye Belle'

direct descendent of 'Queen Elizabeth', it's reasonably heat tolerant, and shows good disease resistance.

David Austin Roses

Description. In general, the David Austin roses are cold hardy down to –20°F (all of Zone 5). They're also relatively heat tolerant, but don't really enjoy full afternoon sunlight when the temperature regularly climbs above 90°F. Disease resistance varies considerably from area to area. With the exception of 'Constance Spry', they flower repeatedly during the season, and all of them are at their best when left alone to develop as the shrubs they are, with no severe pruning or shaping.

History. In the 1950s, David Austin began working at his nursery in Shropshire, England, to develop a new line of roses. His intent was to combine the colors, fragrance, and hardiness of the old European garden roses—the classic gallicas, damasks, and centifolias—with the disease resistance and repetitive flowering of modern roses. His success has been notable, and there is now a large and growing class of shrub roses, known generally as the David Austin English Roses.

In 1961, David Austin released 'Constance Spry', a once-blooming, pink-flowering climber, or large

'Carefree Beauty'

identical rose—is sold as "Katy Road Pink.") Very disease resistant, this rose is a rounded, 4- to 5-foot repeat-flowering shrub with small clusters of large, semidouble, fragrant, open-faced blossoms in rose-pink. And if permitted, it will set a good crop of hips.

'Hawkeye Belle' was released in 1975. It's a wide-growing, 4- to 5-foot shrub with small clusters of large, fragrant double flowers in blush pink to ivory. A

shrub. Then, in 1969, he issued his first catalog, which included seven more new hybrids. Since that time, David Austin's roses have become mainstays in gardens around the world, even in those of fanciers of old or so-called antique roses, among which his are often grouped.

'Belle Story' is an upright, 4-to-5-foot-tall, 2-to-3-foot-wide shrub with small clusters of large mildly double and fragrant, open-faced flowers that are a light pink blend with an island of golden stamens at

'Graham Thomas'

color that's been likened to that of a sweet yellow-meat watermelon. This rose, introduced in 1983, was named for the noted English rosarian and author.

'Heritage' is an erect, 5-foot-tall, 3-foot-wide shrub introduced in 1984. It has small clusters of large, double, cupped flowers that are a pleasing blend of

'Belle Story'

the center. Released in 1984, this rose resents hot summers and heavy clay soils and is mildly susceptible to black spot.

'Graham Thomas' can be grown as a medium shrub or as a small climber because it will grow to a height of from 4 to 12 feet and 3 to 6 feet wide, depending on the site and the climate.

But no matter how or where it's grown, it will present small clusters of large double, cupped flowers that are a unique rich golden yellow and fragrant, a

'Heritage'

light pink shades. These flowers, which are a particular favorite of David Austin, have an intoxicating fragrance reminiscent of damask, myrrh, and lemon.

'Mary Rose' was named for the ill-fated flagship of Henry VIII. 'Mary Rose' was introduced in 1983 and has been one of the more popular English roses for many years. It has very large, double mildly fragrant flowers in rich pink, borne in small clusters on a spreading 4-foot shrub.

'Tamora', also introduced in 1983, is a small, rounded 3-foot shrub. Its flowers appear in small clusters and have a strong myrrh fragrance. They're double, medium-size (2 to 3 inches), and cup-shaped, with a color that is an apricot or dark golden yellow in the center, paling to a light yellow at the perimeter.

'Mary Rose'

'Wife of Bath'

'Tamora'

'The Wife of Bath' was introduced in the first David Austin catalog in 1969. And it continues to be one of his more popular varieties. It's a small, bushy, 3-foot plant with small clusters of medium-size, very double, strongly myrrh-scented flowers that are a pleasing blend of rich- to pale-pink colors. This is one of the more disease-resistant David Austin roses.

Other Shrub Roses

There are many other types and lines of shrub roses to choose from, with varying degrees of cold and heat tolerances and disease resistance. Among the best of the modern shrub roses are the Simplicity roses developed by the Jackson & Perkins company in the United States and the Parkland and Explorer series of hardy roses from Agriculture Canada. Also in that category of desirable roses are many of the Town and Country roses from Poulsen of Denmark, the Generosa roses from Guillot fils of France, and the Meidiland and Romantica roses from the French house of Meilland. In addition, there are several other well-known and popular, individual varieties.

'Carefree Delight' is a member of the Meidiland series of roses developed by Alain Meilland of Antibes, France. It was released in Europe in 1991 as 'Bingo Meidiland' and in the United States in 1993 under what was believed to be a more marketable name. It's

'Carefree Delight'

a 3-to-4-foot-tall-and-wide spreading shrub with 2½-inch, barely fragrant, single or slightly semidouble flowers that are a pleasing pink blend with a white eye. 'Carefree Delight' is cold hardy to –10°F (Zone 5) with a little protection.

Ramblers and Climbers

Description. There is no such thing as a true climbing rose—in the sense that a rose doesn't have tendrils or some other means of grasping a support and pulling itself up. Any rose must be tied to its trellis, arbor, or tree if it's to continue to climb or even remain in place. Even so, there are whole groups of roses that are commonly called climbing roses.

Climbing roses are of two types, that is, ramblers and climbers. The chief difference between the two is that ramblers, which are mostly older antique or species roses, have long, thin, limber canes. And climbers have long, stiff, generally thicker canes. In either case, a climbing rose is nothing more than a bush rose with extra-long canes — or a rose with canes long enough that you can tie it up to some structure and grow it as a climber.

Ramblers are generally quite vigorous, resistant to diseases, and tolerant of heat and cold. But most of them are once-flowering. Climbers, on the other hand, are mostly sports of bush or shrub roses or otherwise cultivated long-caned hybrids. Many of them are relatively disease resistant, and most are repeat-flowering. However, with only a few exceptions, a climbing sport of a bush or shrub rose won't flower nearly as much as its parent. And some of them, for all practical purposes, are once-flowering.

Cold hardiness is a special consideration for once-flowering ramblers and climbers. Because they invariably flower on wood ripened the previous season, the upper growth must be just as hardy as are the roots and the canes near the ground. Otherwise, if there is too much winter dieback, there won't be much wood remaining to flower. So, the long canes of some roses will require some sort of protection if they're to be grown in regions with winter temperatures that approach their limit of cold tolerance.

'Altissimo' (meaning "highest") is a 10-foot-tall, disease-resistant, large-flowered climber introduced in 1966 by Delbart-Chabert of Paris, France. Its large, slightly fragrant cupped flowers, borne singly and in

'America'

'Altissimo'

clusters, have five to seven broad, crimson-scarlet petals. It's quite heat tolerant and cold hardy to –10°F (all of Zone 6).

'America' was developed by Bill Warriner of Jackson & Perkins and introduced in the bicentennial year of 1976. It's a 12-foot, large-flowered climber with an interesting characteristic. If it's pruned back or otherwise reduced in height, it will seldom again grow taller than about 7 feet. It's reasonably disease-resistant and hardy to –20°F (all of Zone 5), and it tolerates hot summer temperatures. Its medium to large double salmon pink flowers are presented in small, loose clusters throughout most of the season. They are fragrant.

'Cherokee' (*Rosa laevigata*) is the state flower of Georgia and has naturalized in favorable locations throughout the South.

Brought from China in 1759, this prickly, evergreen, once-flowering rambler will soar to a height of 15 feet or more. It flowers for about three weeks very early in the season with large, single, mildly fragrant flowers that have broad, creamy white petals and prominent golden stamens. It's spiny, pear-shaped hips are light orange at first, becoming a more brownish shade as they mature.

'Cherokee' is extremely disease resistant but unsuited for those locales where winter temperatures drop below 15°F (colder than Zone 7b). Because 'Cherokee' flowers so early in the season, it is possible to lose many of the flowers to an unusually late freeze.

'Cherokee'

'**Lady Banks, Yellow**' (*R. banksiae* var. *lutea*) was brought to England in 1824 by John Parks. It's similar to the white-flowering 'Lady Banks' in many respects but has some significant differences. It is almost thorn-

'Lady Banks, Yellow'

less, with small double yellow flowers, and is hardy to the normal minimum 5°F in Zone 7b.

'*New Dawn*' is said to be the large-flowered climber

against which all other climbing roses are judged. It was a sport of 'Dr. W. Van Fleet', a 1910 *Rosa wichuraiana* hybrid, that was found and introduced in 1930 by Henry Dree of the Somerset Rose Nursery of New Brunswick, New Jersey. At that time, it received U. S.

'New Dawn'

patent No. 0001, as America's first patented plant.

This rose is disease resistant, is cold hardy to –25F (Zone 4b), grows to a height of 12 to 15 feet, and flowers well all season, with individual blooms or small clusters. The flowers of 'New Dawn' are large, double, fragrant, and a cameo pink that soon fades to a pale flesh pink.

Miniature Roses

Description. Miniature roses are the rose world's version of bonsai—but without the work necessary to keep them small. They're miniature in every way, including flowers, leaflets, stems, and canes. Most will be in the range of from 6 to 18 inches tall, but a few varieties with diminutive flowers and leaves will soar to 3 feet or more. And, of course, there are several climbing varieties. In any case, miniature roses provide everyone with the opportunity of having a rose garden, even if the only space available is a sunny windowsill.

You can plant miniature roses in the garden just like any other rose, but they're used more often as container plants in pots, in window boxes, and even in hanging baskets. They're not really indoor plants, but you can grow them inside if you provide them with six hours of daily sunlight, good air circulation, and a relative humidity of at least 40 percent — and keep an eye out for infestations of spider mites. You can provide sufficient air circulation with an open window or with a fan.

'Palmetto Sunrise', a new miniature rose

And adequate humidity can be achieved by setting the container on a bed of wet gravel.

Miniatures are generally grown on their own roots and are quite cold hardy, tolerating temperatures as low as −10°F (into Zone 5) when protected with a heavy mulch. Of course, container plants can and should be brought inside when temperatures are low enough to freeze the container through and through. But even indoor plants need a period of dormancy, so they should be subjected to enough frosty temperatures to force that state. Then, any leafless, container-ized rose can be wintered indoors in an unheated space. Just make sure the soil is never allowed to dry out completely.

In terms of overall charm and dependability, there is little difference between the many miniature roses now available. Almost without exception, they're hardy, vigorous, disease-resistant shrubs and small climbers. Some varieties may flower more aggressively than others. But other than that, there is little else that will set any one of them aside from the others.

History. It's believed that the origin of today's miniature roses goes back to a carefully cultured Chinese garden rose known as *R. chinensis* var. *minima* or *Rosa semperflorens* var. *minima*, which was first introduced in the West in 1810. Another later, but still early parent seems to have been what is now known as 'Rouletii' (*Rosa rouletii*), a floriferous little rose discovered growing in window boxes in the Swiss villages of Mauborget and Onnens. The first such rose was found by a Major Roulet, a surgeon in the Swiss army during World War I, and the second was retrieved after the war by Henri Correvon, owner of a nursery in Geneva.

The first real achievements in the development of new miniature roses came from the work of the Spanish hybridizer Pedro Dot Martinez in the 1930s and '40s. Jan de Vink of Boscoop, Holland, added several new varieties in the 1950s.

Since then, Harmon Saville of Rowley, Massachusetts, Ernest Schwartz of Kingsville, Maryland, Ralph Moore of Visalia, California, and Ernest Williams of Dallas, Texas, have added many important new varieties. This group of breeders has been largely responsible for the continued popularity of miniature roses.

Collectively, these six men can, therefore, be considered as the godfathers of today's miniature roses, although many of the well-known breeders of normal-sized roses are also now engaged in developing new varieties and new strains.

'Jeanne Lajoie'

'Jeanne Lajoie' is a disease-resistant, robust, vigorous climbing miniature that will cover a trellis 8 feet tall and 3 feet wide. Developed in 1975 by E. P. Sima, it has small, double, high-centered, slightly fragrant rich pink flowers in impressive numbers.

'Minnie Pearl' was developed in 1982 by Harmon Saville of Rowley, Massachusetts, and named for the

star of the Grand Ole Opry. Its flowers are light pink, with a darker reverse. They appear in clusters on an upright shrub only 1½ feet tall. Small and beautifully shaped, double, and mildly fragrant, they're the reason that this is among the highest-rated miniature roses.

'Starina' has been referred to as the 'Peace' of miniature roses because of the classical form of its small,

'Starina'

'Minnie Pearl'

double, exhibition-quality scarlet-orange flowers, which are slightly fragrant. An erect shrub only 1½ feet tall, it was introduced in 1965 by Meilland.

Hardiness

Plants thrive in an environment that approximates their native habitat. For many years, plants have been labeled with their USDA (United States Department of Agriculture) hardiness zone rating, which indicates their tolerance to cold. All of the plants listed in this book are labeled with their USDA Hardiness Zone rating.

Although the USDA ratings are a good starting point, several factors can affect their accuracy. For example, city temperatures tend to be 5° to 10°F warmer than those of the surrounding countryside, raising the hardiness rating of a city garden by a full zone.

Every garden has microclimates that may be warmer or cooler or drier or more humid. The longer you garden in one location, the more familiar you will become with its microclimates. A hardiness rating of "Zones 4 or 5–7 or 8," suggests that the plant may survive the winter cold with protection in the warmer parts of Zone 4, but is safer in Zone 5. And, that same plant may need shade to protect it from the sun's heat in Zone 8, but is more likely to thrive in Zone 7. A plant that is surviving, but not thriving is under stress, and therefore more vulnerable to pests and diseases. Don't be dissuaded from growing a plant at the extremes of its stated cold tolerance. But be prepared to give that plant more attention.

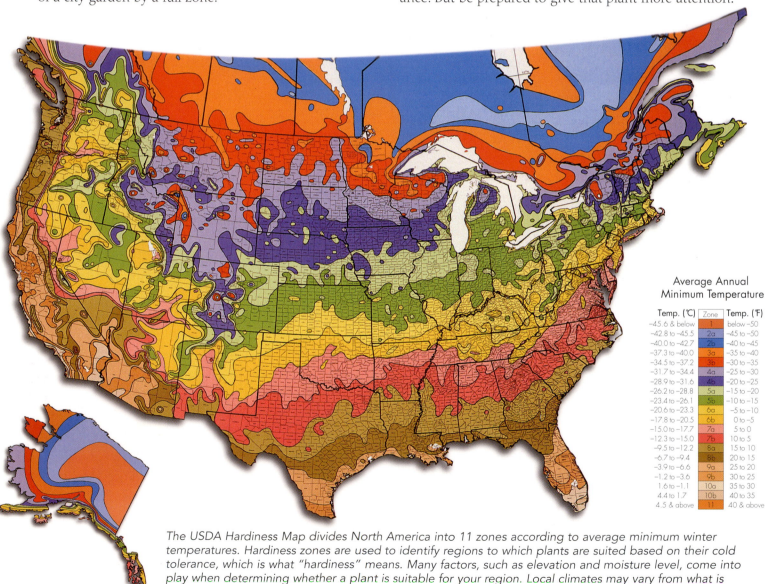

Average Annual Minimum Temperature

Temp. (°C)	Zone	Temp. (°F)
−45.6 & below	1	below −50
−42.8 to −45.5	2a	−45 to −50
−40.0 to −42.7	2b	−40 to −45
−37.3 to −40.0	3a	−35 to −40
−34.5 to −37.2	3b	−30 to −35
−31.7 to −34.4	4a	−25 to −30
−28.9 to −31.6	4b	−20 to −25
−26.2 to −28.8	5a	−15 to −20
−23.4 to −26.1	5b	−10 to −15
−20.6 to −23.3	6a	−5 to −10
−17.8 to −20.5	6b	0 to −5
−15.0 to −17.7	7a	5 to 0
−12.3 to −15.0	7b	10 to 5
−9.5 to −12.2	8a	15 to 10
−6.7 to −9.4	8b	20 to 15
−3.9 to −6.6	9a	25 to 20
−1.2 to −3.6	9b	30 to 25
1.6 to −1.1	10a	35 to 30
4.4 to 1.7	10b	40 to 35
4.5 & above	11	40 & above

The USDA Hardiness Map divides North America into 11 zones according to average minimum winter temperatures. Hardiness zones are used to identify regions to which plants are suited based on their cold tolerance, which is what "hardiness" means. Many factors, such as elevation and moisture level, come into play when determining whether a plant is suitable for your region. Local climates may vary from what is shown on this map. Contact your local Cooperative Extension Service for recommendations for your area.

Heat Tolerance

Researchers have recently discovered that plants begin to suffer cellular damage at temperatures over 86°F (30°C). The American Horticultural Society's Heat-Zone Map divides the country into 12 zones, based on the average number of days each year that a given region experiences "heat days," or temperatures over 86°F. The zones range from Zone 1 (no heat days) to Zone 12 (210 heat days).

In the near future, plants will be labeled with four numbers to indicate cold hardiness and heat tolerance. For example, a tulip may be 3–8, 8–1. If you live in USDA Zone 7 and AHS Zone 7, this label indicates that you can leave tulips outside in your garden all year.

It will take several years for most garden plants to be labeled reliably for heat tolerance. Unusual seasons with fewer or more hot days than normal will invariably affect results. The AHS Heat-Zone ratings assume that adequate water is supplied to the roots of the plant at all times. The accuracy of the coding can be substantially distorted by a lack of water, even for a brief period in the life of the plant.

Both the Cold-Hardiness Zone Map and the Heat-Zone Map are tools. After growing plants in one place for several years, gardeners will know what plants they can and cannot successfully grow.

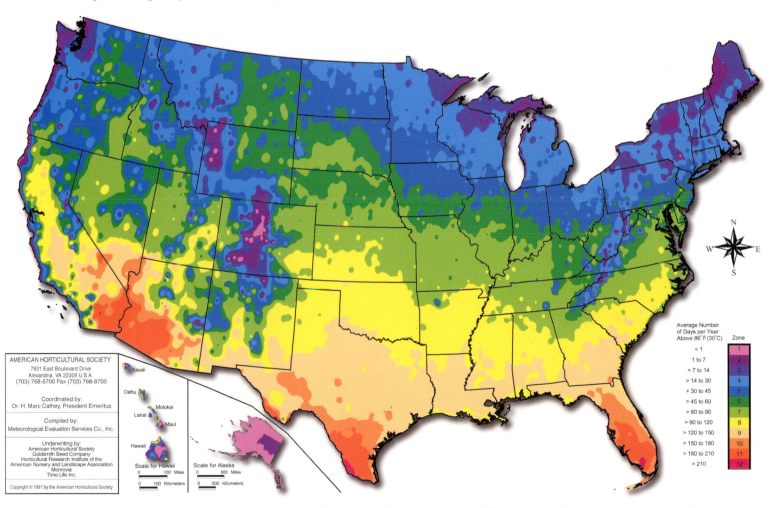

The American Horticultural Society Heat-Zone Map divides the United States into 12 zones based on the average annual number of days a region's temperatures climb above 86°F (30°C), the temperature at which the cellular proteins of plants begin to experience injury. Introduced in 1998, the AHS Heat-Zone Map holds significance, especially for gardeners in southern and transitional zones. Nurseries, growers, and other plant sources will gradually begin listing both cold hardiness and heat tolerance zones for plants, including grass plants. Using the USDA Plant Hardiness map, which can help determine a plant's cold tolerance, and the AHS Heat-Zone Map, gardeners will be able to safely choose plants that tolerate their region's lowest and highest temperatures.

Glossary

Air layering. An asexual propagation method in which roots are stimulated to grow from an aboveground portion of a stem that is still attached to the plant.

Amendments. Organic and inorganic materials that improve aeration, structure, drainage, and nutrient-holding capacity of soil.

Budded rose. A rose that was propagated by budding. With this propagation method, a bud from one rose is grafted onto the rootstock of another.

Bud union. The swollen area where one or more buds were grafted onto a rootstock.

Bud wood. Canes of a selected cultivar, variety, or species from which buds are taken for the purpose of propagating that same type of rose.

Cane. A main shoot of a rose that usually starts near the roots.

Climber. When referring to roses, a rose plant with very long, usually thick, stiff canes that can be trained upright through the use of supports and ties.

Cross (referring to plant breeding). Generally refers to the pollination of a flower by pollen from a plant of a different cultivar or variety.

Crown. The part of the plant where roots and stem meet.

Cultivar. Short for *culti*vated *var*iety. A plant variety developed in cultivation rather than occurring in nature. Cultivar names are usually enclosed in single quotation marks.

Cutting. A plant part (usually a stem or leaf section) that is removed from the mother plant and placed in water or another medium while it develops roots and becomes a new plant.

Dormant period. The time when a plant's growth naturally slows, often after flowering or during the winter months of a year.

Double flower. Flowers having 25 (some say 35) or more petals. Very double roses have 75 or more petals and resemble pom-poms. *See* Single flower and Semidouble flower.

Epsom salts. Magnesium sulfate, often used to supply magnesium.

Feeder root. Thin, fibrous plant roots that gather water and nutrients from the soil.

Fish emulsion. A fertilizer made from byproducts of fish processing. The average analysis is 4-1-1 with 5 percent sulfur.

Fruiting bodies (referring to fungi). The structures on which spores of a fungus form and grow.

Full-spectrum insecticide. A toxin that kills insects indiscriminately.

Genus. A group of closely related species that share similar characteristics and probably evolved from the same ancestors. Genus names are italicized and capitalized. *Plural* genera.

Grafting. A method of propagation that involves attaching a section of one plant onto another in such a way that they grow together. Grafting is usually done to create a plant with more desirable overall characteristics than either of the parent plants.

Hardpan. A compacted layer under the soil surface that prevents water from draining or roots from penetrating it. Hardpans may be natural but are more often caused by poor tillage practices that destroy the soil structure.

Humic acid. An organic acid formed during the decomposition of organic matter.

Humus. A material derived from the almost completely decomposed remains of organic matter. Humus buffers soil acidity and alkalinity, holds water and nutrients, improves soil aggregation and structure, and contains many compounds that enhance plant growth.

Hybrid. A plant resulting from crossbreeding parent plants that belong to different varieties or cultivars, species, or sometimes even genera. Hybrids are indicated by a multiplication sign (X) between the genus and species name or the designation F_1 or F_2.

Indigenous. Native to a particular area or region.

Inoculant. A soil additive that contains nitrogen-fixing bacteria or other microorganisms.

Lateral. Branch arising from a main cane or stem.

Leaf axil. The upper angle at which a leaf joins a stem.

Leaflet. One section of a compound leaf. The leaf begins where the leafstalk attaches to the rose cane. Leaves can have from 3 leaflets to more than over 15 but usually have only 5 to 7.

Loam. A soil type that contains varying amounts of clay, silt, and sand. Loam is the ideal soil for gardening because it tends to drain well and is fertile and moisture retentive.

Macronutrients. Elements required in large quantities by plants for proper nutrition. Nitrogen (N), phosphorus (P), and potassium (K) are generally considered macronutrients. Some soil scientists consider calcium (Ca), magnesium (Mg), and sulfur (S) as macronutrients, although these elements are most commonly described as *minor nutrients. See* Micronutrients.

Microbes. Also known as *microorganisms.* These organisms, which are too small to see with the naked eye, include plants, animals, fungi, viruses, and bacteria.

Microbial action. Life processes of microorganisms, such as the breakdown of organic matter for food.

Micronutrients. Elements required in small quantities by plants for proper nutrition. These include boron (B), chlorine (Cl), cobalt (Co), copper (Cu), iron (Fe), manganese (Mn), molybdenum (Mo), and zinc (Zn). Also known as *trace elements*.

Microorganisms. Also known as *microbes.* These organisms, which are too small to see with the naked eye, include plants, animals, fungi, viruses, and bacteria.

Modern Rose. Any rose belonging to a class that came into being after 1867. According to the American Rose Society (ARS), there are eight major classes of Modern Roses: floribundas, grandifloras, hybrid teas, large-flowered climbers, miniatures, polyanthas, ramblers, and shrubs. *See* Old Garden Rose.

Mycorrhiza fungi. Fungi that have a symbiotic relationship with the roots of certain plants. Mycorrhizae feed on carbohydrates from the plant, and in return supply some elements, such as phosphorus and magnesium, to the plant.

Nematodes. Microscopic wormlike organisms. A few species are detrimental to plants or animals, but many more are benign or beneficial to plants.

Nitrogen fixation. The conversion of atmospheric nitrogen to a form that can be used by plants.

Neutral. Having a pH of 7. *See* pH.

N-P-K ratio. The percentage of nitrogen (N), phosphorus (P), and potassium (K) present in a fertilizer.

Old Garden Rose. Any rose variety or cultivar belonging to a rose class that existed in 1867. According to the American Rose Society, there are 15 classes of Old Garden Roses, including albas, bourbons, centifolias, chinas, damasks, gallicas, moss roses, noisettes, and portlands. *See* Modern Rose.

Once-blooming. Flowering once a year—as compared to repeat-bloomers, which bloom more than once a year. *See* Repeat-blooming.

Own-root rose. A rose that grows on its own roots. *See* Budded rose.

Pegging. Training long-caned roses as ground covers by securing their canes to the ground, generally around the crown of the plant.

Perc test. Short for percolation test. A simple procedure that measures soil drainage. In this test, you monitor how much time it takes for water to drain out of a hole.

pH. The measure of a soil's hydrogen content on a scale of 1 to 14, with 7 considered neutral. A pH above 7 is considered alkaline, and a pH below 7 is considered acidic. Soil pH affects availability of nutrients to plants.

Pheromone. A substance produced by animals or insects that stimulates a certain behavior by other members of the same species. In the garden, pheromones are used to lure insects into traps.

Plant patent. The exclusive right to control the vegetative propagation, use, and sale of a specific plant for 17 to 20 years. The U.S. Patent and Trademark Office grants plant patents.

Rambler. A long-caned rose that can be trained to grow on a trellis or other support.

Remontant. A rose that blooms continuously throughout a season. Also referred to as repeat-blooming.

Repeat-blooming. Flowering more than once a year.

Rooting hormone. A liquid or powder that encourages stems to form roots.

Rootstock. A rose variety used for the roots of a budded plant. Rootstocks are chosen for particular qualities such as disease resistance or tolerance of particular environmental conditions.

Root zone. The area of soil where roots from a particular plant are growing.

Semidouble flower. Flowers with more than 11 petals but fewer than 25.

Silt. Soil particles that are much finer than sand, though coarser than clay. Silt is fairly fertile, compacts easily, and feels slippery.

Single flower. A rose with a single row of 5 petals. Some people consider roses with up to 10 or 11 petals as single flowers. *See* Double flower and Semidouble flower.

Soil layering. A method of propagation in which a section of a stem is slit and buried in the soil to root while it is still attached to the mother plant.

Soluble salt. A nutrient salt that is soluble in water.

Species. A group of plants that shares many characteristics and can interbreed freely. The species name follows the genus name, is italicized, and is not capitalized.

Sport. A natural mutation.

Stratification. Alternate cooling and warming of seeds. Some seeds require a period of freezing followed by a period of warming, while others need to be exposed to temperatures of 40°F or below followed by warming.

Sucker. A stem arising from the rootstock of a woody plant.

Systemic. Taken up by the entire plant or animal system. A pesticide is considered systemic when every cell of the plant contains the material.

Trace elements. Elements required in small quantities by plants for proper nutrition, also called micronutrients. *See* Micronutrients.

Subject Index

Note: Page numbers in italic type indicate photographs and illustrations.

Plant Index

Note: Page numbers in italic type indicate photographs and illustrations.

Photo Credits

CHAPTER 1 *page 8:* John Glover *page 9:* John Glover *page 10:* Derek Fell *page 11:* top left John Glover; *top right* Friedrich Strauss/The Garden Picture Library; *bottom* Jerry Pavia *page 12:* top left Field Roebuck; *top right* Lamontagne/The Garden Picture Library; *bottom* John Glover *page 14:* top Clay Perry/The Garden Picture Library; *bottom* Sunniva Harte/The Garden Picture Library *page 15:* Walter Chandoha *page 16:* Linda Burgess/ The Garden Picture Library *page 17:* all Jerry Pavia *page 18:* top left David Cavagnaro; *top right & bottom* Jerry Pavia *page 19:* all Jerry Pavia *page 20:* all Jerry Pavia *page 21:* left Walter Chandoha; *right* Neil Soderstrom **CHAPTER 2** *page 22:* Ron Evans/The Garden Picture Library *page 23:* Photos Horticultural *page 24:* Derek Fell *page 25:* all Neil Soderstrom *page 26:* all Neil Soderstrom *page 27:* Neil Soderstrom *page 28:* all Neil Soderstrom *page 29:* Neil Soderstrom *page 30:* Neil Soderstrom *page 32:* Friedrich Strauss/The Garden Picture Library *page 33:* left Lamontagne/The Garden Picture Library; *right* Nigel Cattlin/Photo Researchers *page 34:* left Dr. Jeremy Burgess/Photo Researchers; *center top & center bottom* Kim Taylor/Bruce Coleman, Inc.; *right top* Manfred Kage/Peter Arnold, Inc.; *right bottom* Dr. Jeremy Burgess/Photo Researchers *page 35:* left David Phelps/Photo Researchers; *center top* Tony Brain/Photo Researchers; *center bottom* Oliver Meckes/Photo Researchers; *right* Catriona Tudor Erler *page 36:* Neil Soderstrom *page 37:* all Neil Soderstrom *page 38:* all Neil Soderstrom *page 39:* all Neil Soderstrom *page 40:* all Neil Soderstrom *page 41:* all Neil Soderstrom **CHAPTER 3** *page 42:* Marianne Majerus/The Garden Picture Library *page 43:* Neil Soderstrom *page 44:* top Neil Soderstrom; *bottom* John Glover *page 45:* John Glover *page 46:* top & center Derek Fell; *bottom* D. Cavagnaro *page 47:* top Neil Soderstrom/Michael Cady; *bottom* Jerry Pavia *page 48:* Neil Soderstrom *page 49:* all Neil Soderstrom/Michael Cady *page 50:* all Neil Soderstrom/Michael Cady *page 51:* Derek Fell *page 52:* all Neil Soderstrom/Michael Cady **CHAPTER 4** *page 54:* Ron Evans/The Garden Picture Library *page 55:* Derek Fell *page 56:* top Mayer/Le Scanff/The Garden Picture Library; *bottom* John Glover *page 57:* top John Miller/The Garden Picture Library, *bottom* Derek Fell *page 58:* top John Glover; *bottom* Derek Fell *page 59:* John Glover *page 60:* top Field Roebuck; *bottom* Walter Chandoha *page 61:* top Mayer/LeScanff/The Garden Picture Library; *bottom left* Derek Fell; *bottom right box* Neil Soderstrom *page 62:* left Field Roebuck; *right top & bottom* Derek Fell *page 63:* top Walter Chandoha; *bottom* Field Roebuck **CHAPTER 5** *page 64:* Brigitte Thomas/The Garden Picture Library *page 65:* Neil Soderstrom *page 66:* left Neil Soderstrom; *right* Walter Chandoha *page 67:* top Neil Soderstrom; *bottom* S.J. Krasemann/Peter Arnold, Inc. *page 68:* top Walter Chandoha; *bottom* Neil Soderstrom *page 69:* top Derek Fell, *bottom left & right* D. Cavagnaro; *page 70:* left John Glover; *right* Derek Fell *page 71:* top Field Roebuck; *bottom* Derek Fell *page 72:* top Walter Chandoha; *bottom* Derek Fell *page 73:* Neil Soderstrom *page 75:*

Derek Fell *page 76:* top David Askham/The Garden Picture Library; *bottom* Walter Chandoha *page 77:* all Neil Soderstrom *page 78:* top Derek Fell; *bottom* Neil Soderstrom *page 79:* top left Jerry Pavia; *top right* Alan and Linda Detrick; *bottom* Ron Evans/The Garden Picture Library **CHAPTER 6** *page 80:* Derek Fell *page 81:* Neil Soderstrom *page 82:* all Neil Soderstrom *page 83:* Alan and Linda Detrick *page 84:* top Andrew Syred/Photo Researchers; *bottom* Hans Pfletschinger/Peter Arnold, Inc. *page 85:* left Derek Fell; *center & right* Neil Soderstrom *page 86:* Crandall and Crandall *page 87:* top left Neil Soderstrom; *top right & bottom* Derek Fell *page 88:* top left Neil Soderstrom; *top right* Jerry Pavia; *bottom* Alan and Linda Detrick *page 89:* all Field Roebuck *except top left courtesy* Dr. George Philly *page 90:* top Nigel Cattlin/Holt Studios/Photo Researchers; *bottom* Alan and Linda Detrick *page 91:* top left Nigel Cattlin/Holt Studios/Photo Reseachers; *bottom left* Michael Gadomski/Photo Researchers; *right* Nigel Cattlin/Holt Studios/Photo Researchers *page 92:* left Alan and Linda Detrick; *right* Crandall and Crandall *page 93:* left Alan and Linda Detrick; *top right* Nigel Cattlin/Holt Studios/Photo Researchers; *bottom right* Michael Gadomski/Photo Researchers *page 94:* left Alan and Linda Detrick; *right* Crandall and Crandall *page 95:* top left Richard Carton/Photo Researchers; *top right* D. Cavagnaro; *bottom* E.R. Degginger/Photo Researchers **CHAPTER 7** *page 96:* Lynne Brotchie/The Garden Picture Library *page 97:* D. Cavagnaro *page 98:* Walter Chandoha **Chapter 8** *page 104:* Photos Horticultural *page 105:* Jerry Pavia *page 106:* top Lamontagne/The Garden Picture Library; *bottom* D. Cavagnaro *page 107:* top John Glover; *bottom* Derek Fell *page 108:* left D. Cavagnaro; *right* Neil Soderstrom *page 109:* Friedrich Strauss/The Garden Picture Library *page 110:* left Howard Rice/The Garden Picture Library; *right* John Glover *page 111:* Saxon Holt *page 112:* all Field Roebuck *except top right* Alan and Linda Detrick *page 113:* all Field Roebuck *page 114:* all Field Roebuck *page 115:* all Field Roebuck *page 116:* Field Roebuck *page 117:* all Field Roebuck *except bottom left* Jerry Pavia *page 118:* John Glover *page 119:* all Field Roebuck *except inset* Walter Chandoha *page 120:* Jerry Pavia *page 121:* left Field Roebuck; *top & bottom right* Jerry Pavia *page 123:* left Alan and Linda Detrick; *right* John Glover *page 124:* left Jerry Pavia; *right* Alan and Linda Detrick *page 125:* all Jerry Pavia *except top left* Alan and Linda Detrick *page 126:* Jerry Pavia *page 128:* John Glover *page 129:* all Alan and Linda Detrick *page 130:* top Jerry Pavia; *bottom* Alan and Linda Detrick *page 131:* top left Walter Chandoha; *bottom left* Jerry Pavia; *right* Neil Soderstom *page 132:* all Alan and Linda Detrick *except bottom left* John Glover *page 133:* Field Roebuck *page 134:* left Field Roebuck; *right* Jerry Pavia *page 135:* all Jerry Pavia *page 136:* all Jerry Pavia *page 137:* top & bottom left Neil Soderstrom; *right* Jerry Pavia *page 138:* all Jerry Pavia *page 139:* Jerry Pavia *page 140:* left Neil Soderstrom; *right* Jerry Pavia *page 141:* left Field Roebuck, *top right* Jerry Pavia; *bottom right* John Glover *page 142:* all Field Roebuck *page 143:* Neil Soderstrom *page 144:* left John Glover; *right* Jerry Pavia *page 145:* top & bottom left Field Roebuck; *right* John Glover *page 146:* Jerry Pavia *page 147:* top left Field Roebuck; *bottom left & right* Jerry Pavia

All artwork by the masterful hand of Mavis Torke.

Have a home gardening, decorating, or improvement project? Look for these and other fine
Creative Homeowner books wherever books are sold.

An impressive guide to garden design and plant selection. More than 600 color photos. 320 pp.; 9"×10"
BOOK #: 274615

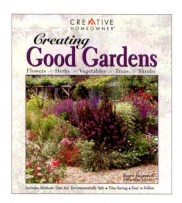

How to prepare, cultivate, and harvest a successful garden. Over 400 color photos. 176 pp.; 9"×10"
BOOK #: 274244

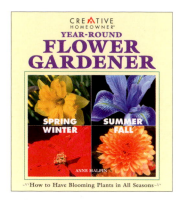

A four-season step-by-step guide to growing flowers. Over 500 photos & illustrations. 224 pp.; 9"×10"
BOOK #: 274791

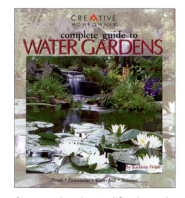

A comprehensive tool for the aspiring water gardener. Over 400 color photos. 208 pp.; 9"×10"
BOOK #: 274452

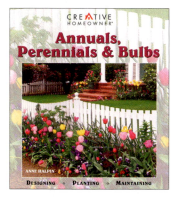

Lavishly illustrated with portraits of over 100 flowering plants; more than 500 photos. 208 pp.; 9"×10"
BOOK #: 274032

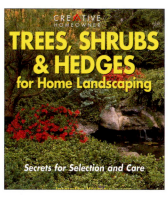

How to select and care for landscaping plants. Over 500 illustrations. 208 pp.; 9"×10"
BOOK #: 274238

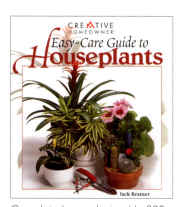

Complete houseplant guide 200 readily available plants; more than 400 photos. 192 pp.; 9"×10"
BOOK #: 275243

Six Regions: Northeast (274618); Mid-Atlantic (274537); Southeast (274762); Midwest (274385); Northwest (274334); California (274267). 400 illustrations each.

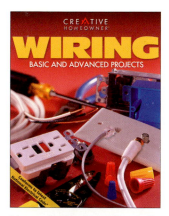

New, updated edition of best-selling house wiring manual. Over 700 color photos. 256 pp.; 8¹⁄₂"×10⁷⁄₈"
BOOK #: 277049

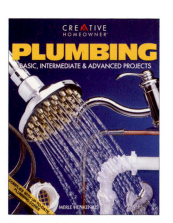

The complete manual for plumbing projects. Over 750 color photos and illustrations. 272 pp.; 8¹⁄₂"×10⁷⁄₈"
BOOK #: 278210

How to work with space, color, pattern, texture. Over 400 photos. 288 pp.; 9"×10"
BOOK #: 279672

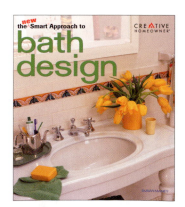

All you need to know about designing a bath. Over 260 color photos. 208 pp.; 9"×10"
BOOK #: 279234

For more information, and to order direct, call 800-631-7795; in New Jersey 201-934-7100.
www.creativehomeowner.com